T0021364

The Little Book for Moms

The
LITTLE BOOK
for
MOMS

STORIES, RECIPES, GAMES, *and* MORE

▲adamsmedia
New York   London   Toronto   Sydney   New Delhi

Adams Media
An Imprint of Simon & Schuster, Inc.
57 Littlefield Street
Avon, Massachusetts 02322

ISBN 978-1-5072-1002-4
eISBN 978-1-4405-8784-9

Printed in the United States of America.

10   9   8   7   6   5   4   3   2   1

Contains material adapted and abridged from *The Everything® Soup, Stew, & Chili Cookbook* by Belinda Hulin, copyright © 2009 by Simon & Schuster, Inc., ISBN 13: 978-1-60550-044-7; *The Everything® Cooking for Kids Book*, copyright © by Simon & Schuster, Inc., ISBN 13: 978-1-60550-665-4; *The Everything® Cookies & Brownies Cookbook* by Marye Audet, copyright © 2009 by Simon & Schuster, Inc., ISBN 13: 978-1-60550-125-3; *The Everything® Classic Recipes Cookbook* by Lynette Rohrer Shirk, copyright © 2006, Simon & Schuster, Inc., ISBN 13: 978-1-59337-690-1; *365 Toddler Activities That Inspire Creativity* by Joni Levine, MEd, copyright © 2012 by Simon & Schuster, Inc., ISBN 13: 978-1-4405-5074-4; *The Everything® Big Book of Party Games* by Carrie Sever; *The Everything® Mother Goose Book* by June Rifkin, copyright © 2001 by Simon & Schuster, Inc., ISBN 13: 978-1-58062-490-9, *The Little Book for Girls* by M.L. Stratton, copyright © 2011 by Simon & Schuster, Inc., ISBN 13: 978-1-4405-2896-5; *The Everything® Pizza Cookbook* by Belinda Hulin, copyright © 2007 by Simon & Schuster, Inc., ISBN 13: 978-1-59869-259-4; and *The Everything® Fairy Tales Book* by Amy Peters, copyright © 2001 by Simon & Schuster, Inc., ISBN 13: 978-1-58062-546-3.

"*Moms hold their children's hands for a moment, but hold their hearts for a lifetime.*"

—UNKNOWN

INTRODUCTION

The Little Book for Moms is the perfect collection of goodies for you to share with your children. After all, some of your kids' favorite childhood memories will come from the many things you teach them as you play, talk, and snuggle together:

- *Silly nursery rhymes.*
- *Warm, gooey chocolate chip cookies.*
- *Homemade play dough.*
- *Unforgettable bedtime stories.*

On these pages, you'll find a timeless collection of stories, songs, quotes, hands-on activities, recipes, and more—all of which help create magical memories your children will remember forever. Whether it's a recipe for mouthwatering apple pie, a fun song to sing during playtime, or a bedtime story to send your little ones off to sleep, you'll turn to this treasury again and again.

Old Mother Hubbard

Old Mother Hubbard
Went to the cupboard
To give the poor dog a bone:
When she came there
The cupboard was bare,
And so the poor dog had none.

She went to the baker's
To buy him some bread;
When she came back
The dog was dead!

She went to the undertaker's
To buy him a coffin;
When she came back
The dog was laughing.

She took a clean dish
to get him some tripe;
When she came back
He was smoking his pipe.

She went to the alehouse
To get him some beer;
When she came back
The dog sat in a chair.

She went to the tavern
For white wine and red;
When she came back
The dog stood on his head.

She went to the fruiterer's
To buy him some fruit;
When she came back
He was playing the flute.

She went to the tailor's
To buy him a coat;
When she came back
He was riding a goat.

She went to the hatter's
To buy him a hat;
When she came back
He was feeding her cat.

She went to the barber's
To buy him a wig,
When she came back
He was dancing a jig.

She went to the cobbler's
To buy him some shoes;
When she came back
He was reading the news.

She went to the seamstress
To buy him some linen;
When she came back
The dog was spinning.

She went to the hosier's
To buy him some hose;
When she came back
He was dressed in his clothes.

The Dame made a curtsy,
The dog made a bow;
The Dame said, Your servant;
The dog said, Bow-wow.

This wonderful dog
Was Dame Hubbard's delight,
He could read, he could dance,
He could sing, he could write;
She gave him rich dainties
Whenever he fed,
And erected this monument
When he was dead.

What Does Little Birdie Say?

BY ALFRED, LORD TENNYSON

What does little birdie say
In her nest at peep of day?
Let me fly, says little birdie,
Mother, let me fly away.
Birdie, rest a little longer,
Till thy little wings are stronger.
So she rests a little longer,
Then she flies away.

What does little baby say,
In her bed at peep of day?
Baby says, like little birdie,
Let me rise and fly away.
Baby, sleep a little longer,
Till thy little limbs are stronger.
If she sleeps a little longer,
Baby too shall fly away.

Little Girl

Little girl, little girl, where have you been?
Gathering roses to give to the Queen.
Little girl, little girl, what gave she you?
She gave me a diamond as big as my shoe.

Cinderella

ADAPTED FROM THE STORY BY THE BROTHERS GRIMM

 NCE UPON A TIME, there was a beautiful girl named Cinderella, who lived with her two stepsisters and stepmother. The stepmother didn't like Cinderella and frequently nagged and scolded her. She made Cinderella do all of the housework.

She had to do all the laundry, all the dishes, and all the cleaning and scrubbing and mending and washing. Despite all this hard work, and the ragged dress she was forced to wear, Cinderella remained kind and optimistic.

One day it was announced that the king had decided to give a ball in honor of his son, the prince. Invitations were sent out to all the young, unmarried girls in the kingdom. Cinderella and her two stepsisters were invited.

Immediately, the stepmother purchased fancy gowns for her daughters, hoping the prince would fall in love with one of them.

Cinderella, of course, was put to work altering the gowns, taking up the hems, and letting out the waists (for her stepsisters were a bit plump).

"Oh, Cinderella," teased the older stepsister, "wouldn't you like to come to the ball?"

Cinderella turned away so her stepsisters wouldn't see the tears in her eyes.

Both stepsisters looked at each other and laughed merrily at the thought of their dirty servant stepsister standing in rags at the ball.

At last the stepsisters were ready, and their carriage pulled up before the front door. Cinderella waved and watched the carriage roll down the street until it was completely out of sight. Then the poor girl burst into tears.

"Why are you crying, child?" said a voice.

Cinderella looked down and saw a tiny, sparkling woman no larger than a teacup standing on the table. "Who are you?" the teary-eyed girl asked.

"I am your Fairy Godmother," said the little woman. "Why are you so sad?"

But Cinderella was too sad to respond.

"You wish you could go to the ball?" The Fairy Godmother finally asked.

"Yes," wept Cinderella. "But I am too poor and too ugly, and everyone would laugh."

"Nonsense," laughed the fairy. "You are beautiful and kind and have all you need. I'll just give you a little help."

"Okay," Cinderella said.

"First, we'll need a pumpkin," said the tiny fairy.

Cinderella brought a pumpkin in from the garden, and the Fairy Godmother gently touched it with her wand. Instantly the pumpkin was transformed into a jeweled coach.

Next, her wand transformed mice into prancing horses to draw the carriage. Some frogs became footmen, and two rats became the coachman and the coach driver.

"Now," said the Fairy Godmother, "you have your carriage. We must see to your gown." She touched Cinderella with her wand. Instantly the ragged dress became a stunning white gown of silk, with beads and pearls and diamonds glittering everywhere. And on her feet were a pair of glass slippers, the most beautiful shoes Cinderella had ever seen.

"Now, go to the ball," said the Fairy Godmother. "But be sure to leave before midnight. At the last stroke of midnight, the coach will be a pumpkin again, the horses will become mice, the coachmen rats, and the footmen will be frogs. And," she added, "your gown will turn back into rags."

So, Cinderella went to the ball in her magic carriage. When she arrived, the prince hurried to greet her. As she stepped from the coach, he gave her his hand and led her into the great hall.

When the two made their entrance, the crowd fell silent. So beautiful a pair was the prince and the strange girl that no one could say a word.

Then, Cinderella and the prince began to waltz.

"What a fine dancer she is," said the stepmother, not recognizing the young girl.

"Her dress is better than mine," sulked the older stepsister.

"Her shoes are nicer than mine," hissed the younger one.

"Quiet, you two," snarled the stepmother, as Cinderella and the prince waltzed by. All three women smiled and waved at the prince, but he had eyes only for Cinderella.

The hours passed like minutes. Cinderella danced and talked with the prince. Then she heard the clock sound the hour of twelve. Terrified that she might be discovered, she had time only to kiss the prince softly on the cheek and hurry from the palace. She rushed down the steps, hopped into her coach, and was gone in an instant.

Cinderella ran away so quickly that she didn't even realize one of her slippers had fallen off. It was picked up by the prince who had turned to follow the girl whose name he hadn't even learned.

At the last stroke of midnight, just as they were out of sight of the palace, the coach and horses and coachmen and footmen changed back into a pumpkin and rats and mice and frogs.

The next morning, her stepsisters told Cinderella all about the ball. They said that the most beautiful princess had appeared and apparently stolen the prince's heart.

That afternoon, a proclamation was issued that the prince himself would be visiting every house in the town to find the owner of the missing glass slipper.

The prince had tried the slipper on all the princesses and duchesses in the court, but none of their feet could fit into it. He then began going to the houses of everyone in the kingdom.

The two stepsisters knew that he would soon come to their house. They fluttered and twittered about.

"Calm down," shouted the stepmother.

The doorbell rang. "Open the door for the prince."

"Welcome, Your Highness," giggled the first stepsister.

The prince frowned, but he asked the two girls to remove their shoes.

The stepsisters tried to make the shoe fit. They shoved and pried and pushed and squeezed and shoved again, but the slipper refused to take hold on their large, bumpy feet.

At last, Cinderella peeked her head around the corner. "May I try?" she asked meekly.

"You?" scoffed the stepmother.

"That's just the cleaning girl," said the older stepsister.

"Let her try," said the prince.

Cinderella sat down in the chair, and the prince lifted the slipper to her foot. It fit beautifully.

"Are you my Princess?" the prince asked.

"I am," Cinderella said happily.

"She can't be!" cried the stepmother.

"Impossible!" shouted the two stepsisters.

From her pocket, Cinderella pulled the other glass slipper and slipped it onto her other foot.

Just then, her Fairy Godmother appeared and touched her with her magic wand. In an instant, Cinderella was clothed in a gown even more beautiful than the one she had worn to the ball.

The prince took Cinderella's hand and led her off to the palace, where they were married in splendor and lived happily ever after.

The stepsisters and stepmother still live together in a rather unkempt home.

Old King Cole

Old King Cole
Was a merry old soul,
And a merry old soul was he;
He called for his pipe,
And he called for his bowl,
And he called for his fiddlers three!
And every fiddler, he had a fine fiddle,
And a very fine fiddle had he.
"Twee tweedle dee, tweedle dee," went the fiddlers.
Oh, there's none so rare
As can compare
With King Cole and his fiddlers three.

MAKE YOUR OWN PLAY DOUGH

Making play dough is a simple and fun activity to try with your children on a rainy afternoon. They can help with the recipe and enjoy hours of fun shaping and molding their very own play dough! Don't forget to store your play dough in an airtight container when you're done having fun.

WHAT YOU'LL NEED:

2 cups flour

2 cups warm water

1 cup salt

2 tablespoons vegetable oil

1 tablespoon cream of tartar

Food coloring gel (if desired)

1. Mix all of the ingredients (except for the food coloring) together in a pot on the stove over low heat.
2. As you stir, the dough will thicken and then pull away from the sides to the center.
3. Continue to stir and cook until the dough is no longer sticky, but has a dry, dough-like texture.
4. Remove the dough so it can cool, and then knead the dough until there are no more lumps.
5. Now you are ready to color the play dough, if you'd like. Separate the dough into pieces and roll the pieces into balls. Then poke a hole into the center and use this hole to put in a few drops of dye. (This way the food coloring won't come into direct contact with your skin until you've worked it into the dough. You could use plastic wrap or disposable gloves to work the food coloring through as well.) Knead the dough to distribute the dye, adding more food coloring until the desired color is reached.

The Owl and the Pussy-Cat

BY EDWARD LEAR

The Owl and the Pussy-Cat went to sea
In a beautiful pea-green boat:
They took some honey, and plenty of money
Wrapped up in a five-pound note.
The Owl looked up to the stars above,
And sang to a small guitar,
"O lovely Pussy, O Pussy, my love,
What a beautiful Pussy you are,
You are,
You are!
What a beautiful Pussy you are!"

Pussy said to the Owl, "You elegant fowl,
How charmingly sweet you sing!
Oh! let us be married; too long we have tarried:
But what shall we do for a ring?"
They sailed away, for a year and a day,
To the land where the bongtree grows;
And there in a wood a Piggy-wig stood,
With a ring at the end of his nose,
His nose,
His nose,
With a ring at the end of his nose.

"Dear Pig, are you willing to sell for one shilling
Your ring?" Said the Piggy, "I will."
So they took it away, and were married next day
By the Turkey who lives on the hill.
They dined on mince and slices of quince,
Which they ate with a runcible spoon;
And hand in hand, on the edge of the sand.
They danced by the light of the moon,
The moon,
The moon,
They danced by the light of the moon.

"*Motherhood:
All love begins
and ends there.*"

—ROBERT BROWNING

HOW TO SAY "I LOVE YOU" IN DIFFERENT LANGUAGES

You probably say "I love you" countless times a day. Why not mix it up once in a while with a foreign language version?

- Afrikaans: Ek het jou lief
- Albanian: Te dua
- Armenian: Yes kez si'rumem
- Cantonese: Ngo oi ney
- Creole: Mi aime jou
- Danish: Jeg elsker dig
- Dutch: Ik hou van jou
- English: I love you
- Filipino: Iniibig kita
- Finnish: Mina rakastan sinua
- French: Je t'aime
- German: Ich liebe dich
- Greek: S'agapo
- Hawaiian: Aloha wau `iâ `oe
- Hungarian: Szeretlek te'ged
- Icelandic: Eg elska thig
- Indonesian: Saya cinta padamu
- Irish/Gaelic: Taim i' ngra leat

- Italian: Ti amo
- Japanese: Kimi o ai shiteru
- Korean: Dangsinul saranghee yo
- Malaysian: Saya cinta mu
- Mandarin: Wo ay ni
- Norwegian: Jeg elsker deg
- Polish: Kocham cie
- Portuguese (Brazilian): Eu to amo
- Romanian: Te iuboco
- Russian: Ya lyublyu tycbya
- Spanish: Te amo
- Swahili: Nakupenda
- Swedish: Jag älskar dig
- Ukrainian: Ya tebe kokhaju
- Vietnamese: Toi yeu em

The Story of Goldilocks and the Three Bears

NCE UPON A TIME, there was a little girl named Goldilocks. She went for a walk in the forest. Pretty soon, she came upon a house. She knocked and, when no one answered, she walked right in.

At the table in the kitchen, there were three bowls of porridge. Goldilocks was hungry. She tasted the porridge from the first bowl.

"This porridge is too hot!" she exclaimed.

So, she tasted the porridge from the second bowl.

"This porridge is too cold," she said.

So, she tasted the last bowl of porridge.

"Ahhh, this porridge is just right," she said happily and she ate it all up.

After she'd eaten the three bears' breakfasts she decided she was feeling a little tired. So, she walked into the living room where she saw three chairs. Goldilocks sat in the first chair to rest her feet.

"This chair is too big!" she exclaimed.

So she sat in the second chair.

"This chair is too big, too!" she whined.

So she tried the last and smallest chair.

"Ahhh, this chair is just right," she sighed. But just as she settled down into the chair to rest, it broke into pieces!

Goldilocks was very tired by this time, so she went upstairs to the bedroom. She lay down in the first bed, but it was too hard. Then she lay in the second bed, but it was too soft. Then she lay down in the third bed and it was just right. Goldilocks fell asleep.

As she was sleeping, the three bears came home.

"Someone's been eating my porridge," growled the Papa bear.

"Someone's been eating my porridge," said the Mama bear.

"Someone's been eating my porridge and they ate it all up!" cried the Baby bear.

"Someone's been sitting in my chair," growled the Papa bear.

"Someone's been sitting in my chair," said the Mama bear.

"Someone's been sitting in my chair and they've broken it all to pieces," cried the Baby bear.

They decided to look around some more and when they got upstairs to the bedroom, Papa bear growled, "Someone's been sleeping in my bed."

"Someone's been sleeping in my bed, too," said the Mama bear.

"Someone's been sleeping in my bed and she's still there!" exclaimed Baby bear.

Just then, Goldilocks woke up and saw the three bears. She screamed, "Help!" And she jumped up and ran out of the room. Goldilocks ran down the stairs, opened the door, and ran away into the forest. And she never returned to the home of the three bears.

One, Two, Buckle My Shoe

One, two,
Buckle my shoe;
Three, four,
Knock at the door;
Five, six,
Pick up sticks;
Seven, eight,
Lay them straight;
Nine, ten,
A good, fat hen;
Eleven, twelve,
Dig and delve;
Thirteen, fourteen,
Maids a-courting;
Fifteen, sixteen,
Maids in the kitchen;
Seventeen, eighteen,
Maids a-waiting;
Nineteen, twenty,
I've had plenty.

Lavender Blue

Lavender's blue, dilly dilly,
Lavender's green
When you are king, dilly dilly,
I shall be queen
Who told you so, dilly dilly,
Who told you so?
'Twas my own heart, dilly dilly,
That told me so
Call up your friends, dilly dilly
Set them to work
Some to the plough, dilly dilly,
Some to the fork
Some to the hay, dilly dilly,
Some to thresh corn
Whilst you and I, dilly dilly,
Keep ourselves warm
Lavender's blue, dilly dilly,
Lavender's green
When you are king, dilly dilly,
I shall be queen
Who told you so, dilly dilly,
Who told you so?
'Twas my own heart, dilly dilly,
That told me so.

Hush, Little Baby

Hush, little baby, don't say a word.

Papa's gonna buy you a mockingbird

And if that mockingbird won't sing,

Papa's gonna buy you a diamond ring

And if that diamond ring turns brass,

Papa's gonna buy you a looking glass

And if that looking glass gets broke,

Papa's gonna buy you a billy goat

And if that billy goat won't pull,

Papa's gonna buy you a cart and bull

And if that cart and bull turn over,

Papa's gonna buy you a dog named Rover

And if that dog named Rover won't bark

Papa's gonna buy you a horse and cart

And if that horse and cart fall down,

You'll still be the sweetest little baby in town.

MOM'S

CHOCOLATE CHIP COOKIES

There's nothing better than sharing a batch of warm cookies straight out of the oven. This is the recipe everyone craves—a crisp outside with a chewy middle. Take these out of the oven when they are still slightly underdone for best results.

YIELDS 24 COOKIES

INGREDIENTS

½ cup unsalted butter
½ cup vegetable shortening
¾ cup sugar
¾ cup brown sugar
2 eggs

1 tablespoon vanilla extract
2¼ cups flour
1 teaspoon baking soda
2 cups chocolate chips

1. Preheat oven to 350°F. Lightly grease cookie sheets.
2. Cream butter, shortening, sugar, and brown sugar until fluffy. Add eggs one at a time; beat well after each egg is added. Beat in vanilla.
3. Combine dry ingredients; stir into butter mixture.
4. Carefully fold in chocolate chips.
5. Drop by teaspoonfuls about 2" apart on cookie sheets. Bake 8–10 minutes. Allow to cool on cookie sheets 10 minutes before removing.

"*If evolution really works, how come mothers only have two hands?*"

—MILTON BERLE

Mary Had a Little Lamb

Mary had a little lamb
Its fleece was white as snow,
And everywhere that Mary went
The lamb was sure to go.

He followed her to school one day
Which was against the rule
It made the children laugh and play
To see a lamb at school.

And so the teacher turned him out,
But still he lingered near,
And waited patiently about
Till Mary did appear.

"What makes the lamb love Mary so?"
The eager children cry.
"Why, Mary loves the lamb, you know,"
The teacher did reply.

WATCH CLASSIC FAMILY MOVIES

Bad weather? Consider watching one of these all-time favorite family movies.

- *Home Alone*
- *Where the Wild Things Are*
- *The Incredibles*
- *Old Yeller*
- *Annie*
- *E.T. the Extra-Terrestrial*
- *Happy Feet*
- *Bambi*
- *Jumanji*
- *Willy Wonka & the Chocolate Factory*
- *Peter Pan*
- *The Blind Side*
- *Rookie of the Year*
- *Mary Poppins*
- *Mars Needs Moms*
- *Freaky Friday*
- *The Sound of Music*
- *Frozen*
- *Mrs. Doubtfire*

Three Blind Mice

Three blind mice! Three blind mice! Three blind mice!
See how they run! See how they run! See how they run!
They all ran after the farmer's wife,
Who cut off their tails with a carving knife.
Did you ever see such a thing in your life
As three blind mice?
Three blind mice!

This Little Piggy

This little piggy went to market;
This little piggy stayed home;
This little piggy had roast beef;
This little piggy had none;
This little piggy cried, "Wee, wee, wee!
All the way home."

Little Miss Muffet

Little Miss Muffet
Sat on a tuffet,
Eating her curds and whey;
Along came a big spider,
Who sat down beside her,
And frightened Miss Muffet away.

MOM'S

MACARONI AND CHEESE

This is a kids' classic that is not just for kids! Serve it with tomatoes and a green salad for a well-balanced meal. This recipe can be divided into individual portions and frozen before it is baked, and then baked at a later date for a quick weeknight dinner.

SERVES 6

INGREDIENTS

4 tablespoons butter

¼ cup all-purpose flour

1 teaspoon dry mustard

2¾ cups milk

1 teaspoon salt

⅛ teaspoon pepper

Pinch cayenne pepper

3 cups shredded Cheddar cheese

10 ounces elbow macaroni, cooked and drained

1 cup dry bread crumbs

1. Preheat oven to 350°F. Butter a 9" × 13" baking dish.
2. Melt the butter in a medium-sized saucepan. Stir in the flour and dry mustard; cook (stirring) over medium heat for 2 minutes.
3. Add the milk and whisk over medium heat until mixture thickens, whisking constantly to prevent burning on the bottom. Stir in the salt, pepper, and cayenne pepper. Remove from heat.
4. Stir in the cheese and let the mixture sit for a minute. Stir again to smooth out the melted cheese.
5. Pour cooked macaroni into the casserole dish; add cheese sauce. Mix until macaroni is coated with cheese.
6. Sprinkle bread crumbs on top of the casserole and bake for 45 minutes, until browned and bubbly on the edges. Serve warm.

The Real Princess
(The Princess and the Pea)

BY HANS CHRISTIAN ANDERSEN

HERE WAS ONCE A PRINCE who wanted to marry a princess. But she must be a real princess, mind you. So he traveled all round the world, seeking such a one, but everywhere something was in the way. Not that there was any lack of princesses, but he could not seem to make out whether they were real princesses; there was always something not quite satisfactory. Therefore, home he came again, quite out of spirits, for he wished so much to marry a real princess.

One evening a terrible storm came on. It thundered and lightened, and the rain poured down; indeed, it was quite fearful. In the midst of it there came a knock at the town gate, and the old king went out to open it.

It was a princess who stood outside. But O dear, what a state she was in from the rain and bad weather! The water dropped from her hair and clothes, it ran in at the tips of her shoes and out at the heels; yet she insisted she was a real princess.

"Very well," thought the old queen; "that we shall presently see." She said nothing, but went into the bedchamber and took off all the bedding, then laid a pea on the sacking of the bedstead. Having done this, she took twenty mattresses and laid them upon the pea and placed twenty eider-down beds on top of the mattresses.

The princess lay upon this bed all the night. In the morning she was asked how she had slept.

"Oh, most miserably!" she said. "I scarcely closed my eyes the whole night through. I cannot think what there could have been in the bed. I lay upon something so hard that I am quite black and blue all over. It is dreadful!"

It was now quite evident that she was a real princess, since through twenty mattresses and twenty eider-down beds she had felt the pea. None but a real princess could have such delicate feeling.

So the prince took her for his wife, for he knew that in her he had found a true princess. And the pea was preserved in the cabinet of curiosities, where it is still to be seen unless some one has stolen it.

And this, mind you, is a real story.

MAKE A MAGIC WAND

You can make a sparkling wand just like Cinderella's Fairy Godmother's. A star is traditional, but you can cut out any shape your kids want.

WHAT YOU'LL NEED:

An unsharpened pencil

Paints or markers

Glue

Ribbons or glitter

Cardboard

Scissors

1. Decorate the pencil in any way you like. For example, you could tape or glue ribbons to it or cover it with glitter.
2. Cut a star shape out of the cardboard. The star should be about the size of your open hand. Decorate the star in any way you like.
3. Glue the star to the end of the pencil. This may have to dry overnight before it is sturdy enough to use. When your wand is dry, enjoy working your magic.

*"Hundreds of dewdrops
to greet the dawn,
Hundreds of bees in
the purple clover,
Hundreds of butter-
flies on the lawn,
But only one mother the
wide world over."*

—GEORGE COOPER

Hot Cross Buns

Hot cross buns!
Hot cross buns!
One a penny, two a penny,
Hot cross buns!

If you have no daughters,
Give them to your sons.
One a penny, two a penny,
Hot cross buns!

Jack Be Nimble

Jack be nimble, Jack be quick,
Jack jump over the candlestick.

Wee Willie Winkie

Wee Willie Winkie runs through the town,
Upstairs and downstairs, in his nightgown;
Rapping at the window, crying through the lock,
"Are the children in their beds?
It's now eight o'clock."

Baa, Baa, Black Sheep

Baa, baa, black sheep,
Have you any wool?
Yes, sir, yes, sir,
Three bags full:
One for my master,
One for my dame,
And one for the little boy
Who lives down the lane.

Hickory, Dickory, Dock

Hickory, dickory, dock!
The mouse ran up the clock;
The clock struck one,
And down he run,
Hickory, dickory, dock!

Where Has My Little Dog Gone?

Oh where, oh where has my little dog gone?
Oh where, oh where can he be?
With his ears cut short and his tail cut long,
Oh where, oh where can he be?

The Itsy Bitsy Spider

The itsy bitsy spider climbed up the water spout,
Down came the rain and washed the spider out.
Out came the sun and dried up all the rain,
And the itsy bitsy spider climbed up the spout again.

Thumbelina

BY HANS CHRISTIAN ANDERSEN

NCE UPON A TIME there was a woman who wanted a
child. Since these were magical times, she went to a fairy and
asked the little sprite if her wish would be granted.

"Oh, yes," said the fairy. "Here is a barleycorn. Put it into a flower-
pot, and see what happens."

"Thank you," said the woman. So she went home and planted it, and
immediately there grew up a large handsome flower. "It is a beautiful
flower," said the woman, and she kissed the leaves. When she did so, the
flower opened, and within the flower perched a tiny maiden. She was
scarcely half as long as a thumb, and she gave her the name of Thumbelina because she was so small.

Her bed was formed of blue violet-leaves and a walnut shell. One
night, while she lay in her pretty bed, a large, slimy toad crept through
a broken pane of glass, and leaped right upon the table where Thumbelina lay sleeping under her roseleaf quilt. "What a pretty wife she would
make for my son," said the toad, and she took the walnut-shell bed in
which little Thumbelina lay asleep and jumped through the window
with it.

The toad's son was even uglier than his mother, and when he saw
the pretty little maiden in her walnut-shell bed, he could only cry happily, "Croak, croak, croak."

They placed her on a water-lily leaf out in a stream where she couldn't escape, while the toad and her son made plans for a very fancy wedding ceremony.

Thumbelina woke very early in the morning and began to cry when she found where she was, for she could see nothing but water on every side and no way of reaching the land.

Eventually, the toad swam out with her ugly son to the leaf on which they had placed Thumbelina. "Here is my son, he will be your husband, and you will live happily in the marsh by the stream," the toad croaked.

Thumbelina cried because she could not bear to think of living with the old toad and having her ugly son for a husband. The little fishes, who swam about in the water beneath, had seen the toad and heard what she said, so they lifted their heads above the water to look at the little maiden. As soon as they caught sight of her, they saw she was very pretty. It made them very sorry to think that she must go and live with the ugly toads. So they gnawed away at the root of the leaf where Thumbelina was sitting. When they had finished, the leaf floated down the stream.

Thumbelina sailed past many towns. Presently a large beetle flew by, and the moment he caught sight of her, he seized her round her slim waist and flew with her into a tree.

Oh, how frightened little Thumbelina felt when the beetle flew with her to the tree! He seated himself by her side on a large green leaf, gave her some honey from the flowers to eat, and told her she was very pretty. But all of the other beetles turned up and said, "She has only two legs! How ugly that looks."

Then the beetle believed all the others when they said she was ugly and would have nothing more to say to her. He told her she might go where she liked.

During the whole summer, poor little Thumbelina lived quite alone in the wide forest. The summer passed and the autumn; then came the winter, a long, cold winter. She felt so cold. She wrapped herself up in a dry leaf, but it cracked in the middle and could not keep her warm. Finally, she went looking for shelter. She came to the door of a field mouse, who had a little den under the corn-stubble. There dwelt the field mouse in warmth and comfort, with a whole roomful of corn, a kitchen, and a beautiful dining room. Poor little Thumbelina stood before the door just like a little beggar-girl and asked for a crumb of food.

"You poor little creature," said the field mouse, who was really a good, kind field mouse, "come into my warm room and dine with me. We shall have a visitor soon. My neighbor pays me a visit once a week. He is rich. If you could only have him for a husband, you would be well provided for indeed. But he is blind, so you must tell him a pretty story."

But Thumbelina did not feel at all interested in this neighbor, for he was a mole. But, the mole, upon hearing Thumbelina's lovely voice, fell in love with her. He said nothing yet, for he was very cautious.

A short time before, the mole had dug a long passage under the earth, which led from the dwelling of the field mouse to his home. He warned them not to be alarmed at the sight of a dead bird in the passage.

When Thumbelina saw the bird—which was a swallow—she felt very sad. She stooped down and stroked aside the soft feathers that covered the head and kissed the closed eyelids.

That night Thumbelina could not sleep. So she got out of bed and wove a large, beautiful quilt of hay. Then she carried it to the dead bird and spread it over him. Then she laid her head on the bird's breast, but she was alarmed immediately, for it seemed as if something inside the bird went *thump, thump*. It was the bird's heart. He was not really dead, only numb with the cold, and the warmth had restored him to life. Thumbelina trembled for the bird was a great deal larger than herself— she was only an inch high. But she took courage and laid the blanket more thickly over the poor swallow. The next morning she again stole out to see him. He was alive but very weak.

"Thank you, pretty little maiden," said the sick swallow. "I have been so nicely warmed that I shall soon regain my strength and be able to fly about again in the warm sunshine."

The whole winter the swallow remained underground, and Thumbelina nursed him. Neither the mole nor the field mouse knew anything about it, for they did not like swallows. Very soon the springtime came, and the sun warmed the earth. Then the swallow bade farewell to Thumbelina. The swallow asked her if she would go with him; she could sit on his back, but Thumbelina knew it would make the field mouse very sad so she said no.

"Good-bye, then," said the swallow and he flew away.

"You are going to be married, Thumbelina," said the field mouse soon after the swallow left. "My neighbor has asked for you."

As soon as the summer was over, the wedding would take place. But Thumbelina was not at all pleased, for she did not like the tiresome mole.

When autumn arrived the field mouse said to her, "In four weeks the wedding must take place."

Then Thumbelina wept and said she would not marry the disagreeable mole.

"Nonsense," replied the field mouse. "Now don't be stubborn or I shall bite you with my white teeth."

So the wedding day was set, and the mole was to fetch Thumbelina away to live with him, deep under the earth. The poor child was very unhappy at the thought of saying farewell to the beautiful sun. The field mouse had given her permission to stand at the door, so she went to look at the sun once more.

"Farewell, bright sun," she cried.

Tweet, tweet, sounded over her head suddenly. She looked up, and there was the swallow flying close by. As soon as he spied Thumbelina, he was delighted; and then she told him that she didn't want to marry the ugly mole, and to live always beneath the earth, and never to see the bright sun anymore.

"Cold winter is coming," said the swallow, "and I am going to fly away into warmer countries. Will you go with me? Fly now with me, dear little Thumbelina. You saved my life when I lay frozen."

"Yes, I will go with you," said Thumbelina, and she seated herself on the bird's back.

Then the swallow rose in the air and flew over forest and over sea, high above the highest mountains, covered with snow. At last they came to a blue lake, and by the side of it, shaded by trees of the deepest green, stood a palace of dazzling white marble. Vines clustered round its lofty pillars, and at the top were many swallows' nests. One was the home of the swallow that carried Thumbelina.

"This is my house," said the swallow; "but it would not do for you to live there. You must choose for yourself one of those lovely flowers, and I will put you down upon it."

"That will be delightful," she said.

A large marble pillar lay on the ground broken into three pieces. Between these pieces grew the most magnificent white flowers. The swallow flew down with Thumbelina and placed her on one of the broad leaves. But how surprised she was to see in the middle of the flower, a tiny little man, as white and transparent as if he had been made of glass! He had a gold crown on his head and delicate wings at his shoulders, and he was not much larger than Thumbelina herself. He was the angel of the flower. A tiny man and a tiny woman dwell in every flower. This was the king of them all.

The little prince was at first quite frightened of the bird, who was like a giant, compared to such a delicate little guy like himself. But when he saw Thumbelina, he was delighted, and thought her the prettiest little maiden he had ever seen. He asked if she would be his wife and queen over all the flowers.

She said, "Yes," to the handsome prince. Then all the flowers opened, and out of each came a little lady or a tiny lord. They were all so pretty it was quite a pleasure to look at them. Each of them brought Thumbelina a present. The best gift of all was a pair of beautiful wings, which had belonged to a large white fly. They fastened them to Thumbelina's shoulders, so that she might fly happily from flower to flower and visit her new friends.

MAKE DECORATIVE BIRD FEEDERS

Kids of all ages can make this craft! Your kids will be as delighted to make it as the birds will be to eat it, especially if you can watch the birds in action. You can also make a birdfeeder using a pinecone or an empty paper towel roll covered with honey or peanut butter and rolled in birdseed.

WHAT YOU'LL NEED:
A few slices of bread, old or new
Cookie cutter(s)
An egg white and a pastry brush
Birdseed of any variety
A straw
Pieces of ribbon, yarn, or twine

1. Preheat the oven to 350°F. Beat the egg white until frothy in a small bowl, and pour the birdseed into a shallow dish.
2. Use the cookie cutters to make shapes in the slices of bread. With the straw, punch out a hole for the string about ¼" from the edge.
3. Brush the cut outs with the egg whites, and then press them into the birdseed. Bake for about 10 minutes.
4. When cooled, thread the string through the hole and hang in a spot where you can watch the birds enjoy!

Here We Go Round the Mulberry Bush

Here we go round the mulberry bush
The mulberry bush, the mulberry bush
Here we go round the mulberry bush
So early in the morning.

This is the way we wash our clothes
Wash our clothes, wash our clothes
This is the way we wash our clothes
So early Monday morning.

This is the way we iron our clothes
Iron our clothes, iron our clothes
This is the way we iron our clothes
So early Tuesday morning.

This is the way we mend our clothes
Mend our clothes, mend our clothes
This is the way we mend our clothes
So early Wednesday morning.

This is the way we sweep the floor
Sweep the floor, sweep the floor
This is the way we sweep the floor
So early Thursday morning.

This is the way we scrub the floor
Scrub the floor, scrub the floor
This is the way we scrub the floor
So early Friday morning.

This is the way we bake our bread
Bake our bread, bake our bread
This is the way we bake our bread
So early Saturday morning.

This is the way we go to church
Go to church, go to church
This is the way we go to church
So early Sunday morning.

Tom Thumb

BY THE GRIMM BROTHERS

 POOR WOODMAN sat in his cottage one night, smoking his pipe by the fireside, while his wife sat by his side spinning. "How lonely it is, wife," said he, as he puffed out a long curl of smoke, "for you and me to sit here by ourselves, without any children to play about and amuse us while other people seem so happy and merry with their children!" "What you say is very true," said the wife, sighing, and turning round her wheel; "how happy should I be if I had but one child! If it were ever so small—nay, if it were no bigger than my thumb—I should be very happy, and love it dearly." Now—odd as you may think it—it came to pass that this good woman's wish was fulfilled, just in the very way she had wished it; for, not long afterwards, she had a little boy, who was quite healthy and strong, but was not much bigger than my thumb. So they said, "Well, we cannot say we have not got what we wished for, and, little as he is, we will love him dearly." And they called him Thomas Thumb.

They gave him plenty of food, yet for all they could do he never grew bigger, but kept just the same size as he had been when he was born. Still, his eyes were sharp and sparkling, and he soon showed himself to be a clever little fellow, who always knew well what he was about.

One day, as the woodman was getting ready to go into the wood to cut fuel, he said, "I wish I had someone to bring the cart after me, for I want to make haste." "Oh, father," cried Tom, "I will take care of that; the cart shall be in the wood by the time you want it." Then the woodman laughed, and said, "How can that be? you cannot reach up to the horse's bridle." "Never mind that, father," said Tom; "if my mother will only harness the horse, I will get into his ear and tell him which way to go." "Well," said the father, "we will try for once."

When the time came the mother harnessed the horse to the cart, and put Tom into his ear; and as he sat there the little man told the beast how to go, crying out, "Go on!" and "Stop!" as he wanted: and thus the horse went on just as well as if the woodman had driven it himself into the wood. It happened that as the horse was going a little too fast, and Tom was calling out, "Gently! gently!" two strangers came up. "What an odd thing that is!" said one: "there is a cart going along, and I hear a carter talking to the horse, but yet I can see no one." "That is queer, indeed," said the other; "let us follow the cart, and see where it goes." So they went on into the wood, till at last they came to the place where the woodman was. Then Tom Thumb, seeing his father, cried out, "See, father, here I am with the cart, all right and safe! now take me down!" So his father took hold of the horse with one hand, and with the other took his son out of the horse's ear, and put him down upon a straw, where he sat as merry as you please.

The two strangers were all this time looking on, and did not know what to say for wonder. At last one took the other aside, and said, "That little urchin will make our fortune, if we can get him, and carry him about from town to town as a show; we must buy him." So they went up to the woodman, and asked him what he would take for the little man. "He will be better off," said they, "with us than with you." "I won't sell him at all," said the father; "my own flesh and blood is dearer to me than all the silver and gold in the world." But Tom, hearing of the bargain they wanted to make, crept up his father's coat to his shoulder and whispered in his ear, "Take the money, father, and let them have me; I'll soon come back to you."

So the woodman at last said he would sell Tom to the strangers for a large piece of gold, and they paid the price. "Where would you like to sit?" said one of them. "Oh, put me on the rim of your hat; that will be a nice gallery for me; I can walk about there and see the country as we go along." So they did as he wished; and when Tom had taken leave of his father they took him away with them.

They journeyed on till it began to be dusky, and then the little man said, "Let me get down, I'm tired." So the man took off his hat, and put him down on a clod of earth, in a ploughed field by the side of the road. But Tom ran about amongst the furrows, and at last slipped into an old mouse-hole. "Good night, my masters!" said he, "I'm off! mind and look sharp after me the next time." Then they ran at once to the place, and poked the ends of their sticks into the mouse-hole, but all in vain; Tom only crawled farther and farther in; and at last it became quite dark, so that they were forced to go their way without their prize, as sulky as could be.

When Tom found they were gone, he came out of his hiding-place. "What dangerous walking it is," said he, "in this ploughed field! If I were to fall from one of these great clods, I should undoubtedly break my neck." At last, by good luck, he found a large empty snail-shell. "This is lucky," said he, "I can sleep here very well"; and in he crept.

Just as he was falling asleep, he heard two men passing by, chatting together; and one said to the other, "How can we rob that rich parson's house of his silver and gold?" "I'll tell you!" cried Tom. "What noise was that?" said the thief, frightened; "I'm sure I heard someone speak." They stood still listening, and Tom said, "Take me with you, and I'll soon show you how to get the parson's money." "But where are you?" said they. "Look about on the ground," answered he, "and listen where the sound comes from." At last the thieves found him out, and lifted him up in their hands. "You little urchin!" they said, "what can you do for us?" "Why, I can get between the iron window-bars of the parson's house, and throw you out whatever you want." "That's a good thought," said the thieves; "come along, we shall see what you can do."

When they came to the parson's house, Tom slipped through the window-bars into the room, and then called out as loud as he could bawl, "Will you have all that is here?" At this the thieves were frightened, and said, "Softly, softly! Speak low, that you may not awaken anybody." But Tom seemed as if he did not understand them, and bawled out again, "How much will you have? Shall I throw it all out?" Now the cook lay in the next room; and hearing a noise she raised herself up in her bed and listened. Meantime the thieves were frightened, and ran off a little way; but at last they plucked up their hearts, and said, "The little urchin is only trying to make fools of us." So they came back and whispered softly to him, saying, "Now let us have no more of your roguish jokes, but throw us out some of the money." Then Tom called out as loud as he could, "Very well! hold your hands! here it comes."

The cook heard this quite plain, so she sprang out of bed, and ran to open the door. The thieves ran off as if a wolf was at their tails: and the maid, having groped about and found nothing, went away for a light. By the time she came back, Tom had slipped off into the barn; and when she had looked about and searched every hole and corner, and found nobody, she went to bed, thinking she must have been dreaming with her eyes open.

The little man crawled about in the hayloft, and at last found a snug place to finish his night's rest in; so he laid himself down, meaning to sleep till daylight, and then find his way home to his father and mother. But alas! how woefully he was undone! what crosses and sorrows happen to us all in this world! The cook got up early, before daybreak, to feed the cows; and going straight to the hayloft, carried away a large bundle of hay, with the little man in the middle of it, fast asleep. He still, however, slept on, and did not awake till he found himself in the mouth of the cow; for the cook had put the hay into the cow's rick, and the cow had taken Tom up in a mouthful of it. "Good lack-a-day!" said he, "how came I to tumble into the mill?" But he soon found out where he really was; and was forced to have all his wits about him, that he might not get between the cow's teeth, and so be crushed to death. At last down he went into her stomach. "It is rather dark," said he; "they forgot to build windows in this room to let the sun in; a candle would be no bad thing."

Though he made the best of his bad luck, he did not like his quarters at all; and the worst of it was, that more and more hay was always coming down, and the space left for him became smaller and smaller. At last he cried out as loud as he could, "Don't bring me any more hay! Don't bring me any more hay!"

The maid happened to be just then milking the cow; and hearing someone speak, but seeing nobody, and yet being quite sure it was the same voice that she had heard in the night, she was so frightened that she fell off her stool, and overset the milk pail. As soon as she could pick herself up out of the dirt, she ran off as fast as she could to her master the parson, and said, "Sir, sir, the cow is talking!" But the parson said, "Woman, thou art surely mad!" However, he went with her into the cow-house, to try and see what was the matter.

Scarcely had they set foot on the threshold, when Tom called out, "Don't bring me any more hay!" Then the parson himself was frightened; and thinking the cow was surely bewitched, told his man to kill her on the spot. So the cow was killed, and cut up; and the stomach, in which Tom lay, was thrown out upon a dunghill.

Tom soon set himself to work to get out, which was not a very easy task; but at last, just as he had made room to get his head out, fresh ill-luck befell him. A hungry wolf sprang out, and swallowed up the whole stomach, with Tom in it, at one gulp, and ran away.

Tom, however, was still not disheartened; and thinking the wolf would not dislike having some chat with him as he was going along, he called out, "My good friend, I can show you a famous treat." "Where's that?" said the wolf. "In such and such a house," said Tom, describing his own father's house. "You can crawl through the drain into the kitchen and then into the pantry, and there you will find cakes, ham, beef, cold chicken, roast pig, apple-dumplings, and everything that your heart can wish."

The wolf did not want to be asked twice; so that very night he went to the house and crawled through the drain into the kitchen, and then into the pantry, and ate and drank there to his heart's content. As soon as he had had enough he wanted to get away; but he had eaten so much that he could not go out by the same way he came in.

This was just what Tom had reckoned upon; and now he began to set up a great shout, making all the noise he could. "Will you be easy?" said the wolf; "you'll awaken everybody in the house if you make such a clatter." "What's that to me?" said the little man; "you have had your frolic, now I've a mind to be merry myself"; and he began singing and shouting as loud as he could.

The woodman and his wife, being awakened by the noise, peeped through a crack in the door; but when they saw a wolf was there, you may well suppose that they were sadly frightened; and the woodman ran for his axe, and gave his wife a scythe. "Do you stay behind," said the woodman, "and when I have knocked him on the head you must rip him up with the scythe." Tom heard all this, and cried out, "Father, father! I am here, the wolf has swallowed me." And his father said, "Heaven be praised! we have found our dear child again"; and he told his wife not to use the scythe for fear she should hurt him. Then he aimed a great blow, and struck the wolf on the head, and killed him on the spot! and when he was dead they cut open his body, and set Tommy free. "Ah!" said the father, "what fears we have had for you!" "Yes, father," answered he; "I have traveled all over the world, I think, in one way or other, since we parted; and now I am very glad to come home and get fresh air again." "Why, where have you been?" said his father. "I have been in a mouse-hole—and in a snail-shell—and down a cow's throat—and in the wolf's belly; and yet here I am again, safe and sound."

"Well," said they, "you are come back, and we will not sell you again for all the riches in the world."

Then they hugged and kissed their dear little son, and gave him plenty to eat and drink, for he was very hungry; and then they fetched new clothes for him, for his old ones had been quite spoiled on his journey. So Master Thumb stayed at home with his father and mother, in peace; for though he had been so great a traveler, and had done and seen so many fine things, and was fond enough of telling the whole story, he always agreed that, after all, there's no place like HOME!

Brahms's Lullaby (Lullaby and Goodnight)

Lullaby and goodnight, with roses bedight

With lilies o'er spread is baby's wee bed

Lay thee down now and rest, may thy slumber be blessed

Lay thee down now and rest, may thy slumber be blessed

Lullaby and goodnight, thy mother's delight

Bright angels beside my darling abide

They will guard thee at rest, thou shalt wake on my breast

They will guard thee at rest, thou shalt wake on my breast.

Rock-A-Bye Baby

Rock-a-bye baby, on the tree top,
When the wind blows the cradle will rock;
When the bough breaks the cradle will fall;
And down will come baby, cradle and all.

PETER PIPER PICKED A PUMPKIN PUDDING

This is a sweet and delicious pudding that's good any time of the year! Pumpkin contains fiber, vitamin A, vitamin C, and potassium—so your little ones will get more than just a yummy dessert.

SERVES 8–10

INGREDIENTS

2 (12-ounce) boxes frozen butternut squash

1 (15-ounce) can solid pumpkin

2 eggs, beaten

2 tablespoons sugar

½ teaspoon ginger

½ teaspoon cinnamon

1 teaspoon vanilla extract

Nonstick cooking spray

1. Preheat oven to 375°F.
2. Cook squash according to package directions.
3. In a medium mixing bowl, mix squash, pumpkin, eggs, sugar, seasonings, and vanilla extract.
4. Spray nonstick cooking spray into a medium pie pan.
5. Bake 45 minutes.

Peter Piper

Peter Piper picked a peck of pickled peppers;
A peck of pickled peppers Peter Piper picked.
If Peter Piper picked a peck of pickled peppers,
Where's the peck of pickled peppers Peter Piper picked?

"All that I am or ever hope to be, I owe to my angel mother."

—ABRAHAM LINCOLN

BALL-IN-A-BOX PAINTING

It's like magic—when you open the box, you'll find a picture painted inside!

WHAT YOU'LL NEED:
Scissors
White or light-colored bond paper
Shoebox with a lid
Masking tape
Tempera paints
Shallow pie tins
Ping-Pong or golf balls

1. Cut a piece of paper to fit the bottom of the box. Tape it securely in place.
2. Pour small amounts of paint into the pie tins. Show your toddler how to dip a ball into the paint.
3. Have him place the paint-covered ball into the shoebox. Cover the box with the lid.
4. Let your child gently roll and shake the box around.
5. Remove the ball. Repeat with as many other balls and colors as desired

Rapunzel

ADAPTED FROM THE STORY BY THE BROTHERS GRIMM

NCE UPON A TIME, a man and a woman lived in a snug home near a beautiful walled garden. They were quite happy, except for one thing: They had no children. Finally, after years of waiting, the wife became pregnant.

Oddly enough, the woman found that she craved something called rampion, a green for making salads. Rampion is also called Rapunzel. Her husband spied some inside the walls of the garden next door. Although he'd never met the person who tended the garden, he thought he'd try his luck at getting some for his hungry wife.

That night, by the light of the moon, he climbed over the stone wall into the beautiful garden and picked a small basketful of the rampion. He rushed back over the wall and gave the leaves to his wife who ate them happily.

The next night she craved more, so he was forced to make another trip over the wall into the neighbor's garden. This time though, he was caught in the act—by an old, warty fairy.

"How dare you steal into my garden and take my rampion?" she hissed.

"Oh, I'm sorry," he said. "But I felt I had to. My wife is pregnant and craving your delicious rampion. You're quite a gardener!"

"I think she'll have a daughter," said the fairy. "I was planning to kill you, but I will spare you on one condition."

"You name it," said the man.

"Your wife shall have as much rampion as she likes, and you shall live," said the fairy, "but when your daughter is twelve years old, you will give her to me. Then, you are never to see her again."

The man agreed, because he was afraid the fairy would kill him otherwise. When he told his wife, she cried, but she agreed that her husband really had no choice.

When the child was born, the hideous fairy appeared and gave her the name Rapunzel. Then, she vanished and did not reappear, as promised, until the girl's twelfth birthday.

"I have come for you, Rapunzel," said the fairy.

The girl agreed to go because she did not want her father to die.

The fairy shut Rapunzel up in a stone tower in the middle of a forest. There was no door to this tower, and no stairs. There was only one window high at the top, far too high for any ladder to reach.

When the fairy wanted to go up, she stood at the bottom and cried in her hoarse voice, "Rapunzel, Rapunzel, let down your golden hair."

Rapunzel, who had spectacularly long hair, would drop her luxurious locks down to the fairy standing far below. Then the woman would climb up the hair.

After a few years, a prince riding through the forest happened to hear a beautiful voice singing. He hurried toward the sound and saw the tower. In the window far above, he saw a beautiful girl, singing sweetly to herself.

The prince wanted to climb the tower, but he saw right away that it wasn't possible. There was no door or stairs. He rode home, but every day he came back to the tower and listened to the girl's sweet song and waited for a glimpse of her face in the window.

One day while he was waiting, he saw the fairy arrive and croak, "Rapunzel, Rapunzel, let down your golden hair."

As he watched the wicked woman climb the hair, he came up with a plan to reach the beautiful maiden. The next day when it grew dark, he went to the tower and croaked like the old fairy, "Rapunzel, Rapunzel, let down your golden hair."

Down came the beautiful golden hair, and up he climbed.

As you can imagine, the prince's appearance was a bit of a shock for Rapunzel. The prince reassured her, though, and told her that he had heard her singing for many months and that he had fallen in love with her through her splendid songs. Rapunzel fell in love with him as well. The prince asked her to marry him, and she happily said yes.

"But how will you escape from this prison?" the prince asked.

"Bring a length of silk thread with you every time you visit," Rapunzel said. "I will weave a thread ladder, and when it is ready I will come with you."

So, every evening, the prince returned with a fine silk thread, and as they talked she wove the ladder of silk. Finally, the ladder was finished. It had not been easy hiding it from the old fairy, for she was quite suspicious and questioned Rapunzel harshly about strange human smells in the tower. Rapunzel, however, was able to convince her that nothing was amiss.

One night, by the glowing light of the moon, the prince came to rescue Rapunzel. She hung the delicate ladder from the windowsill and climbed down carefully into the arms of her waiting prince charming! They were married shortly after at the prince's royal residence and lived there very happily.

As for the ugly fairy, to this day she can't understand how Rapunzel escaped. And she's quite vexed about it!

MAKE PAPER DOLLS

Boys and girls alike enjoy making little people to decorate, name, and play with.

WHAT YOU'LL NEED:
Construction paper or card stock
Pencils to draw doll and accessories
Scissors
Craft glue
Markers, colored pencils, or crayons
Old wrapping paper or decorative paper or any sort
Ribbon, yarn, old buttons, sequins, stickers, glitter, scraps of cloth

1. Draw a doll pattern on a piece of construction paper (you can make as many of the same-sized dolls as you want, or make different sized patterns to create a doll family!).
2. Carefully cut out the pattern(s) with scissors.
3. Trace around the doll's body on another sheet of paper (wrapping, decorative, or construction paper) in the shape of clothes for your doll. Don't forget to make tabs on the clothes to fold over the doll's body!
4. Use the ribbon, sequins, etc. to decorate your clothes. You can also create accessories like purses, shoes, and jewelry.

Skip to My Lou

Lou, Lou, skip to my Lou
Lou, Lou, skip to my Lou
Lou, Lou, skip to my Lou
Skip to my Lou, my darlin'!

Fly's in the buttermilk,
Shoo, fly, shoo,
Fly's in the buttermilk,
Shoo, fly, shoo,
Fly's in the buttermilk,
Shoo, fly, shoo,
Skip to my Lou, my darlin'.

Lou, Lou, skip to my Lou
Lou, Lou, skip to my Lou
Lou, Lou, skip to my Lou
Skip to my Lou, my darlin'!

Lost my partner,
What'll I do?
Lost my partner,
What'll I do?
Lost my partner,
What'll I do?
Skip to my Lou, my darlin'.

Lou, Lou, skip to my Lou
Lou, Lou, skip to my Lou
Lou, Lou, skip to my Lou
Skip to my Lou, my darlin'!

I'll find another one,
Prettier, too,
I'll find another one,
Prettier, too,
I'll find another one,
Prettier, too,
Skip to my Lou, my darlin'.

"God could not
be everywhere,
and therefore he
made mothers."

—RUDYARD KIPLING

Sleeping Beauty

NCE UPON A TIME, a baby girl was born into a royal family. To celebrate her arrival, all the fairies in the land were invited to be godmothers. After the baptism, a banquet was planned. Seven places of honor were set with golden dishes and diamond goblets.

At the royal banquet, each of the seven fairy godmothers gave their gifts and advice to the tiny baby. There was great jubilation in the palace until, suddenly, an old, wizened fairy angrily appeared.

"Why is there no place for me?" the old fairy demanded.

No place had been set for the fairy because it was well known that she was not a good fairy. Instead, she practiced mischief and black magic. Enraged at being spurned, she pulled out her magic wand and cackled, "I'll give her a gift she'll never forget. When she turns sixteen, the princess will cut her finger on a spindle, and she will die!" Then the old fairy vanished in a flash of lightning.

The king and queen began to cry, but the seventh fairy godmother urged them not to despair. "Your Majesties, I can't completely undo this curse, but I can make it milder. Instead of dying, when the princess cuts her finger, she and the entire kingdom will fall asleep for a hundred years. All will be awakened by the kiss of a prince."

This brought some comfort to the king and queen. In hopes of thwarting the curse altogether, however, they passed a law forbidding all spindles in their kingdom.

The evil fairy's magic was very powerful, though. On the princess's sixteenth birthday, she was exploring the highest, most isolated turret of the castle, where she found an old woman smiling and spinning golden thread.

"What is that?" the princess asked, because she had never seen a spinning wheel.

"A spindle," said the old woman. "Would you like to see it?"

The princess reached her hand out and cut her finger on the spindle. She immediately fell asleep on the floor. The old woman picked up the princess and placed her on a bed in the room. Then the old lady, who was really the wicked old fairy, vanished in flash of lightning.

At that same instant, everyone in the castle fell into a deep sleep: the king and queen, the animals in the stables, the maids and cooks, even the goose herder in the field.

A hundred years passed and the old castle was overgrown by the trees of the forest.

One day, a prince was lost in this dark forest. He was far from his own kingdom, hungry, and tired. He was just about to give up all hope when he saw the glint of stone in the distance. As he grew near the stone, he was amazed to see the stone made up the wall of a castle. It was quite magnificent despite the vines creeping up along its walls and the huge lawn that was choked with weeds.

He made his way inside and marveled at the inhabitants of the castle, who were all asleep. Guards slept standing at their posts, seamstresses sat sleeping on their stools, cooks stood sleeping in mid-stir, and a sleeping musician sat poised to play the piano. It was a very odd sight, thought the Prince.

As he walked through the castle, he came to the very room where the beautiful princess slept. There on a high bed made of gold and emeralds was the most beautiful girl he had ever seen. The prince leaned forward and kissed the sleeping girl on her forehead.

Just then, the princess's eyes opened, and she looked at the prince as if she'd known him forever.

"Is that you, My Prince?" she whispered. "I've waited so long."

Then, the prince told her that he had loved her from the first moment he'd laid eyes on her. One by one the servants awoke, and they prepared a great wedding feast.

The prince and princess were married that very afternoon and loved each other forever after.

The Three Little Kittens

Three little kittens, they lost their mittens,
And they began to cry,
Oh, mother dear, we sadly fear
That we have lost our mittens.

What! Lost your mittens, you naughty kittens!
Then you shall have no pie.
Mee-ow, mee-ow, mee-ow, mee-ow.
You shall have no pie.

The three little kittens, they found their mittens,
And they began to cry,
Oh, mother dear, see here, see here,
Our mittens we have found.

Put on your mittens, you silly kittens,
And you shall have some pie.
Purr-r, purr-r, purr-r,
Oh, let us have some pie.

The three little kittens, they put on their mittens,
And soon ate up the pie;
Oh, mother dear, we greatly fear
That we have soiled our mittens.

What! Soiled your mittens, you naughty kittens!
Then they began to sigh,
Mee-ow, mee-ow, mee-ow, mee-ow.
They began to sigh.

The three little kittens, they washed their mittens,
And hung them out to dry;
Oh! mother dear, do you not hear
That we have washed our mittens?

What! Washed your mittens, then you're such good kittens.
But I smell a rat close by
Mee-ow, mee-ow, mee-ow, mee-ow.
We smell a rat close by.

"Biology is the least of what makes someone a mother."

—OPRAH WINFREY

PLAY "NEXT LINE, PLEASE"

This is a game that the whole family can play. This a great activity for long plane rides or when you have to wait somewhere.

1. Each person takes a turn by adding a sentence to an evolving story. No one player can have control over what will happen, but the adult may need to keep the story somewhat on track.

2. Your new story may evolve like this:

   Parent: One day there was a bear who . . .

   Child: Lived in a house.

   Parent: This bear was hungry and . . .

   Child: The boy likes toys.

   Parent: So they got together to get lunch and go to the toy store. When they got there they saw

3. Consider having your child draw illustrations for her story.

CHICKEN NOODLE SOUP

Sure, this soup can be prepared with premade broth, leftover chicken, and noodles, but this recipe shows how your mom or grandma probably did it. When it comes to buying and cooking poultry, a "hen" refers to a bird that is older and larger than the typical fryer or broiler. Hens usually weigh 4–6 pounds, in contrast to the 2½–3 pound average fryer. They're more flavorful, but also tougher birds, making them perfect for slow-cooked soups and stews.

SERVES 6

INGREDIENTS

1 stewing hen, about 5 pounds
Water
1 onion, quartered
1 small bunch parsley, rinsed
1 green onion, halved
3 ribs celery, cut in thirds
3 carrots, cut in thirds

1 rib celery, thinly sliced
1 carrot, thinly sliced
1 cup peas
1 cup medium noodles
¼ cup minced parsley
Salt and pepper to taste

1. Rinse hen and remove giblets. Save for another use. Place hen in large Dutch oven with enough water to almost cover. Add onion, parsley, green onion, celery cut in thirds, and carrot cut in thirds. Bring water to a boil over high heat; reduce heat to medium low. Simmer 2 hours. Remove from heat and allow to cool.
2. Carefully remove chicken from broth. Remove breast and thigh meat. Return chicken carcass and skin to broth. Cook over medium-low heat 6–8 hours. Remove from heat. Strain broth through fine sieve.

3. Pour broth into clean soup pot. There should be about 10 cups. Add sliced celery and sliced carrot. Stir in peas. Bring broth to a boil over high heat; add noodles, stirring to disperse. Cook, stirring frequently, until noodles are tender, about 10 minutes. Reduce heat to medium low. Chop or shred reserved chicken meat. Add to broth; simmer 10 minutes. Add parsley.

4. Season with salt and pepper and serve.

The Goose-Girl

BY THE BROTHERS GRIMM

HE KING OF A GREAT LAND DIED, and left his queen to take care of their only child. This child was a daughter, who was very beautiful; and her mother loved her dearly, and was very kind to her. And there was a good fairy too, who was fond of the princess, and helped her mother to watch over her. When she grew up, she was betrothed to a prince who lived a great way off; and as the time drew near for her to be married, she got ready to set off on her journey to his country. Then the queen her mother, packed up a great many costly things; jewels, and gold, and silver; trinkets, fine dresses, and in short everything that became a royal bride. And she gave her a waiting-maid to ride with her, and give her into the bridegroom's hands; and each had a horse for the journey. Now the princess's horse was the fairy's gift, and it was called Falada, and could speak.

When the time came for them to set out, the fairy went into her bed-chamber, and took a little knife, and cut off a lock of her hair, and gave it to the princess, and said, "Take care of it, dear child; for it is a charm that may be of use to you on the road." Then they all took a sorrowful leave of the princess; and she put the lock of hair into her bosom, got upon her horse, and set off on her journey to her bridegroom's kingdom.

One day, as they were riding along by a brook, the princess began to feel very thirsty: and she said to her maid, "Pray get down, and fetch me some water in my golden cup out of yonder brook, for I want to drink." "Nay," said the maid, "if you are thirsty, get off yourself, and stoop down by the water and drink; I shall not be your waiting-maid any longer." Then she was so thirsty that she got down, and knelt over the little brook, and drank; for she was frightened, and dared not bring out her golden cup; and she wept and said, "Alas! what will become of me?" And the lock answered her, and said:

"Alas! alas! if thy mother knew it,

Sadly, sadly, would she rue it."

But the princess was very gentle and meek, so she said nothing to her maid's ill behavior, but got upon her horse again.

Then all rode farther on their journey, till the day grew so warm, and the sun so scorching, that the bride began to feel very thirsty again; and at last, when they came to a river, she forgot her maid's rude speech, and said, "Pray get down, and fetch me some water to drink in my golden cup." But the maid answered her, and even spoke more haughtily than before: "Drink if you will, but I shall not be your waiting-maid." Then the princess was so thirsty that she got off her horse, and lay down, and held her head over the running stream, and cried and said, "What will become of me?" And the lock of hair answered her again:

"Alas! alas! if thy mother knew it,

Sadly, sadly, would she rue it."

And as she leaned down to drink, the lock of hair fell from her bosom, and floated away with the water. Now she was so frightened that she did not see it; but her maid saw it, and was very glad, for she knew the charm; and she saw that the poor bride would be in her power, now that she had lost the hair. So when the bride had done drinking, and would have got upon Falada again, the maid said, "I shall ride upon Falada, and you may have my horse instead"; so she was forced to give up her horse, and soon afterwards to take off her royal clothes and put on her maid's shabby ones.

At last, as they drew near the end of their journey, this treacherous servant threatened to kill her mistress if she ever told anyone what had happened. But Falada saw it all, and marked it well.

Then the waiting-maid got upon Falada, and the real bride rode upon the other horse, and they went on in this way till at last they came to the royal court. There was great joy at their coming, and the prince flew to meet them, and lifted the maid from her horse, thinking she was the one who was to be his wife; and she was led upstairs to the royal chamber; but the true princess was told to stay in the court below.

Now the old king happened just then to have nothing else to do; so he amused himself by sitting at his kitchen window, looking at what was going on; and he saw her in the courtyard. As she looked very pretty, and too delicate for a waiting-maid, he went up into the royal chamber to ask the bride who it was she had brought with her, that was thus left standing in the court below. "I brought her with me for the sake of her company on the road," said she; "pray give the girl some work to do, that she may not be idle." The old king could not for some time think of any work for her to do; but at last he said, "I have a lad who takes care of my geese; she may go and help him." Now the name of this lad, that the real bride was to help in watching the king's geese, was Curdken.

But the false bride said to the prince, "Dear husband, pray do me one piece of kindness." "That I will," said the prince. "Then tell one of your slaughterers to cut off the head of the horse I rode upon, for it was very unruly, and plagued me sadly on the road"; but the truth was, she was very much afraid lest Falada should some day or other speak, and tell all she had done to the princess. She carried her point, and the faithful Falada was killed; but when the true princess heard of it, she wept, and begged the man to nail up Falada's head against a large dark gate of the city, through which she had to pass every morning and evening, that there she might still see him sometimes. Then the slaughterer said he would do as she wished; and cut off the head, and nailed it up under the dark gate.

Early the next morning, as she and Curdken went out through the gate, she said sorrowfully:

"Falada, Falada, there thou hangest!"

and the head answered:

"Bride, bride, there thou gangest!

Alas! alas! if thy mother knew it,

Sadly, sadly, would she rue it."

Then they went out of the city, and drove the geese on. And when she came to the meadow, she sat down upon a bank there, and let down her waving locks of hair, which were all of pure silver; and when Curdken saw it glitter in the sun, he ran up, and would have pulled some of the locks out, but she cried:

"Blow, breezes, blow!

Let Curdken's hat go!

Blow, breezes, blow!

Let him after it go!

O'er hills, dales, and rocks,

Away be it whirl'd

Till the silvery locks

Are all comb'd and curl'd!"

Then there came a wind, so strong that it blew off Curdken's hat; and away it flew over the hills: and he was forced to turn and run after it; till, by the time he came back, she had done combing and curling her hair, and had put it up again safe. Then he was very angry and sulky, and would not speak to her at all; but they watched the geese until it grew dark in the evening, and then drove them homewards.

The next morning, as they were going through the dark gate, the poor girl looked up at Falada's head, and cried:

"Falada, Falada, there thou hangest!"

and the head answered:

"Bride, bride, there thou gangest!

> Alas! alas! if thy mother knew it,
>
> Sadly, sadly, would she rue it."

Then she drove on the geese, and sat down again in the meadow, and began to comb out her hair as before; and Curdken ran up to her, and wanted to take hold of it; but she cried out quickly:

> "Blow, breezes, blow!
>
> Let Curdken's hat go!
>
> Blow, breezes, blow!
>
> Let him after it go!
>
> O'er hills, dales, and rocks,
>
> Away be it whirl'd
>
> Till the silvery locks
>
> Are all comb'd and curl'd!"

Then the wind came and blew away his hat; and off it flew a great way, over the hills and far away, so that he had to run after it; and when he came back she had bound up her hair again, and all was safe. So they watched the geese till it grew dark.

In the evening, after they came home, Curdken went to the old king, and said, "I cannot have that strange girl to help me to keep the geese any longer." "Why?" said the king. "Because, instead of doing any good, she does nothing but tease me all day long." Then the king made him tell him what had happened. And Curdken said, "When we go in the morning through the dark gate with our flock of geese, she cries and talks with the head of a horse that hangs upon the wall, and says:

> 'Falada, Falada, there thou hangest!'

and the head answers:

> 'Bride, bride, there thou gangest!
>
> Alas! alas! if thy mother knew it,
>
> Sadly, sadly, would she rue it.'"

And Curdken went on telling the king what had happened upon the meadow where the geese fed; how his hat was blown away; and how he was forced to run after it, and to leave his flock of geese to themselves.

But the old king told the boy to go out again the next day: and when morning came, he placed himself behind the dark gate, and heard how she spoke to Falada, and how Falada answered. Then he went into the field, and hid himself in a bush by the meadow's side; and he soon saw with his own eyes how they drove the flock of geese; and how, after a little time, she let down her hair that glittered in the sun. And then he heard her say:

"Blow, breezes, blow!
Let Curdken's hat go!
Blow, breezes, blow!
Let him after it go!
O'er hills, dales, and rocks,
Away be it whirl'd
Till the silvery locks
Are all comb'd and curl'd!"

And soon came a gale of wind, and carried away Curdken's hat, and away went Curdken after it, while the girl went on combing and curling her hair. All this the old king saw: so he went home without being seen; and when the little goose-girl came back in the evening he called her aside, and asked her why she did so: but she burst into tears, and said, "That I must not tell you or any man, or I shall lose my life."

But the old king begged so hard, that she had no peace till she had told him all the tale, from beginning to end, word for word. And it was very lucky for her that she did so, for when she had done the king ordered royal clothes to be put upon her, and gazed on her with wonder, she was so beautiful. Then he called his son and told him that he had only a false bride; for that she was merely a waiting-maid, while the true bride stood by. And the young king rejoiced when he saw her beauty, and heard how meek and patient she had been; and without saying anything to the false bride, the king ordered a great feast to be got ready for all his court. The bridegroom sat at the top, with the false princess on one side, and the true one on the other; but nobody knew her again, for her beauty was quite dazzling to their eyes; and she did not seem at all like the little goose-girl, now that she had her brilliant dress on.

When they had eaten and drank, and were very merry, the old king said he would tell them a tale. So he began, and told all the story of the princess, as if it was one that he had once heard; and he asked the true waiting-maid what she thought ought to be done to anyone who would behave thus. "Nothing better," said this false bride, "than that she should be thrown into a cask stuck round with sharp nails, and that two white horses should be put to it, and should drag it from street to street till she was dead." "Thou art she!" said the old king; "and as thou has judged thyself, so shall it be done to thee." And the young king was then married to his true wife, and they reigned over the kingdom in peace and happiness all their lives; and the good fairy came to see them, and restored the faithful Falada to life again.

Sing a Song of Sixpence

Sing a song of sixpence,
A pocket full of rye;
Four and twenty blackbirds
Baked in a pie.
When the pie was opened
The birds began to sing;
Wasn't that a dainty dish
To set before the king?

The king was in his counting house,
Counting out his money;
The queen was in the parlor,
Eating bread and honey.
The maid was in the garden,
Hanging out the clothes;
When down came a blackbird
And snipped off her nose.

"*The mother's heart is the child's schoolroom.*"

—HENRY WARD BEECHER

PLAY "DOUBLE DUTCH"

This timeless playground activity is endless family fun—and great exercise!— once you get the hang of it. For spinners, rhythm is important, along with deciding how fast or slow they'd like to turn the ropes. For the jumper, timing and coordination are essential to learning to jump Double Dutch.

WHAT YOU'LL NEED:

2 jump ropes

At least three people: two turners to swing the ropes, and at least one jumper!

1. First, the turners take the ropes, one in each hand, and hold their hands at waist height, shoulder width apart. They begin swinging the jump ropes simultaneously in opposite directions, their left arms swinging the rope clockwise, their right arms turning the other rope counterclockwise, making large arcs with the ropes. When the left hand is up, the right hand should be down.

2. The jumper then jumps into the ropes when the rope closest to them hits the ground, jumping in at a diagonal angle. (You can start in the middle of the ropes before they start being turned if you find it too difficult to jump in while the ropes are swinging.)

3. The jumper(s) need to move their feet alternately to jump over the ropes as they pass by. You can play to see how many jumps you can do in a certain time, experiment with different freestyle tricks, or jump along to schoolyard Double Dutch rhymes and verses.

JUMP ROPE RHYMES

These jump rope rhymes are perfect for playing Double Dutch!

1. Cinderella, dressed in yellow
   Went upstairs to kiss a fellow
   Made a mistake
   Kissed a snake
   How many doctors
   Did it take?
   1, 2, 3, 4 (continue counting until the jumper misses)

2. Call for the doctor, call for the nurse,
   And call for the lady with the alligator purse!
   In came the doctor, in came the nurse,
   And in came the lady with the alligator purse.
   Out went the doctor, out went the nurse,
   And out went the lady with the alligator purse!

3. All in together, birds of a feather:
   January, February, March, April, May, etc. (each player jumps in during
   the month they were born)

4. Ice cream soda, Delaware Punch,
Tell me the name of my honey-bunch.
A, B, C (continue until the jumper misses)

5. Miss Mary Mack, Mack, Mack,
All dressed in black, black, black,
With silver buttons, buttons, buttons,
All down her back, back, back,
She asked her mother, mother, mother,
For fifty cents, cents, cents,
To see the elephant, elephant, elephant,
Jump the fence, fence, fence,
They jumped so high, high, high,
They touched the sky, sky, sky,
And didn't come back, back, back,
Till the Fourth of July, -ly, -ly.

6. Ice cream, soda pop, cherry on top,
Who's your best friend?
I forgot!
A, B, C (continue until the jumper misses)

The Country Mouse and the City Mouse

NCE UPON A TIME there was a city mouse that, having tired of the hustle and bustle of his neighborhood, took a trip to the country. Once there, he met a country mouse.

They spent the day together and became friends. The country mouse took his new friend into the lush meadows and vegetable gardens. The city mouse sampled all of the vegetables and found them to be very good. Never having seen the beauties of the country, the city mouse was thrilled. But the country mouse's plain food wasn't nearly as fine as his own usual meals of fine cheeses and hams found in the home where he lived.

To thank his friend for the lovely outing, he invited the country mouse to visit him in town. And when the country mouse saw the pantry at his friend's house—full of hams, cheese, oil, flour, honey, jam, and stacks of other delicious goodies—he stood speechless.

After he got over his surprise, he said, "I've never seen anything like it! Are all those wonderful things for eating?"

"Of course!" came the reply. "You're my guest. Dig in!"

So, the pair began to feast. The country mouse tried not to stuff himself, taking small samples of everything, as he wanted to taste each item before finding his tummy full.

"You're the luckiest mouse I've ever met!" said the country mouse. The city mouse was listening with delight to his friend's praise, when suddenly the sound of heavy footsteps interrupted their feast.

"Run for it!" whispered the town mouse to his friend. They were just in time; for within an inch of them was the ungainly foot of the lady of the house. Luckily, the lady went away, and the two mice returned to enjoy their feast.

"It's all right! Come on!" reassured the town mouse. "Don't worry. She's gone. Now let's have some honey! It's delicious! Have you ever tasted it?"

"Yes, once, a long time ago," the country mouse lied, trying to sound casual. But when he tasted it, he couldn't contain his enthusiasm: "Wow! It's scrumptious! By the king of Mice! I've never eaten anything so remarkable in my life!"

Suddenly there came the sound of footsteps, this time thumping heavily. The two mice fled. The man of the house had come to get some bottles; and when he saw the spilt honey, he groaned, "Those rotten mice again! I thought I'd gotten rid of them. I'll send the cat!"

And trembling with fear, the mice hid. This time it was not only the sudden visit that had given them a fright; it was the man's terrifying words. The mice were so scared that they held their breath, making absolutely no sound. Then, since all remained quiet, they began to feel braver and gathered enough courage to venture out. "We can come out now! There's nobody here!" the town mouse whispered.

Suddenly, the pantry door creaked, and the two luckless mice froze in fear. Out of the dim light glowed a pair of horrid, ghostly yellow eyes. But this was no ghost. It was a large cat, searching the room for the mice. The country mouse and the town mouse tiptoed silently back to their hiding place. They wished their pounding hearts would stop beating, for fear the cat would hear the noise they made. But, as luck would have it, the cat discovered a juicy sausage. Forgetting why his master had sent him into the pantry, he stopped to eat it. No longer hungry after that, the cat decided that he might as well leave mouse hunting for another day.

Off he padded to have a nap. Now, as soon as the country mouse realized that all danger was past, he did not lose a second. He hastily shook hands with his friend, saying, "Thanks so much for everything! But I must rush off now! I can't stand all these shocks! I'd far rather sit down to a meal of a few crumbs in peace, in the country, than face a fancy feast, surrounded by danger."

"*The phrase 'working mother' is redundant.*"

—JANE SELLMAN

MOM'S

RETRO BLONDIES

These butterscotch-flavored brownies have been a favorite with kids and adults alike for decades. Sprinkle the tops of the Blondies with some confectioners' sugar just before serving for a sweet touch.

YIELDS 16 BLONDIES

INGREDIENTS

2 cups flour
1 teaspoon baking powder
1 teaspoon salt
¼ teaspoon baking soda
½ cup unsalted butter
1 cup brown sugar, packed

2 eggs
1 teaspoon vanilla
1 cup chocolate chips
1 cup pecans or walnuts,
   optional

1. Preheat oven to 325°F. Grease 9" square pan. (Glass works best for this recipe.)
2. Sift together dry ingredients; set aside. Melt butter and brown sugar together, stirring until smooth. Let cool to room temperature.
3. Add eggs one at a time, beating well after each addition. Stir in vanilla.
4. Fold in dry ingredients, chocolate chips, and nuts (if using) until well blended and there are no streaks of flour in the dough.
5. Bake 30–35 minutes, or until a toothpick inserted in the center comes out with just a few crumbs clinging to it. Cool and cut into squares.

The Ugly Duckling

BY HANS CHRISTIAN ANDERSEN

T WAS SO BEAUTIFUL IN THE COUNTRY. It was the summer time. The wheat fields were golden, the oats were green, and the hay stood in great stacks in the green meadows. The stork paraded about among them on his long red legs, chattering away in Egyptian, the language he had learned from his lady mother.

All around the meadows and cornfields grew thick woods, and in the midst of the forest was a deep lake. Yes, it was beautiful, it was delightful in the country.

In a sunny spot stood a pleasant old farmhouse circled all about with deep canals; and from the walls down to the water's edge grew great burdocks, so high that under the tallest of them a little child might stand upright. The spot was as wild as if it had been in the very center of the thick wood.

In this snug retreat sat a duck upon her nest, watching for her young brood to hatch; but the pleasure she had felt at first was almost gone; she had begun to think it a wearisome task, for the little ones were so long coming out of their shells, and she seldom had visitors. The other ducks liked much better to swim about in the canals than to climb the slippery banks and sit under the burdock leaves to have a gossip with her. It was a long time to stay so much by herself.

At length, however, one shell cracked, and soon another, and from each came a living creature that lifted its head and cried "Peep, peep."

"Quack, quack!" said the mother; and then they all tried to say it, too, as well as they could, while they looked all about them on every side at the tall green leaves. Their mother allowed them to look about as much as they liked, because green is good for the eyes.

"What a great world it is, to be sure," said the little ones, when they found how much more room they had than when they were in the eggshell.

"Is this all the world, do you imagine?" said the mother. "Wait till you have seen the garden. Far beyond that it stretches down to the pastor's field, though I have never ventured to such a distance. Are you all out?" she continued, rising to look. "No, not all; the largest egg lies there yet, I declare. I wonder how long this business is to last. I'm really beginning to be tired of it"; but for all that she sat down again.

"Well, and how are you to-day?" quacked an old duck who came to pay her a visit.

"There's one egg that takes a deal of hatching. The shell is hard and will not break," said the fond mother, who sat still upon her nest. "But just look at the others. Have I not a pretty family? Are they not the prettiest little ducklings you ever saw? They are the image of their father—the good for naught! He never comes to see me."

"Let me see the egg that will not break," said the old duck. "I've no doubt it's a Guinea fowl's egg. The same thing happened to me once, and a deal of trouble it gave me, for the young ones are afraid of the water. I quacked and clucked, but all to no purpose. Let me take a look at it. Yes, I am right; it's a Guinea fowl, upon my word; so take my advice and leave it where it is. Come to the water and teach the other children to swim."

"I think I will sit a little while longer," said the mother. "I have sat so long, a day or two more won't matter."

"Very well, please yourself," said the old duck, rising; and she went away.

At last the great egg broke, and the latest bird cried "Peep, peep," as he crept forth from the shell. How big and ugly he was! The mother duck stared at him and did not know what to think. "Really," she said, "this is an enormous duckling, and it is not at all like any of the others. I wonder if he will turn out to be a Guinea fowl. Well, we shall see when we get to the water—for into the water he must go, even if I have to push him in myself."

On the next day the weather was delightful. The sun shone brightly on the green burdock leaves, and the mother duck took her whole family down to the water and jumped in with a splash. "Quack, quack!" cried she, and one after another the little ducklings jumped in. The water closed over their heads, but they came up again in an instant and swam about quite prettily, with their legs paddling under them as easily as possible; their legs went of their own accord, and the ugly gray coat was also in the water, swimming with them.

"Oh," said the mother, "that is not a Guinea fowl. See how well he uses his legs, and how erect he holds himself! He is my own child, and he is not so very ugly after all, if you look at him properly. Quack, quack! come with me now. I will take you into grand society and introduce you to the farmyard, but you must keep close to me or you may be trodden upon; and, above all, beware of the cat."

When they reached the farmyard, there was a wretched riot going on; two families were fighting for an eel's head, which, after all, was carried off by the cat. "See, children, that is the way of the world," said the mother duck, whetting her beak, for she would have liked the eel's head herself. "Come, now, use your legs, and let me see how well you can behave. You must bow your heads prettily to that old duck yonder; she is the highest born of them all and has Spanish blood; therefore she is well off. Don't you see she has a red rag tied to her leg, which is something very grand and a great honor for a duck; it shows that every one is anxious not to lose her, and that she is to be noticed by both man and beast. Come, now, don't turn in your toes; a well-bred duckling spreads his feet wide apart, just like his father and mother, in this way; now bend your necks and say 'Quack!'"

The ducklings did as they were bade, but the other ducks stared, and said, "Look, here comes another brood—as if there were not enough of us already! And bless me, what a queer-looking object one of them is; we don't want him here"; and then one flew out and bit him in the neck.

"Let him alone," said the mother; "he is not doing any harm."

"Yes, but he is so big and ugly. He's a perfect fright," said the spiteful duck, "and therefore he must be turned out. A little biting will do him good."

"The others are very pretty children," said the old duck with the rag on her leg, "all but that one. I wish his mother could smooth him up a bit; he is really ill-favored."

"That is impossible, your grace," replied the mother. "He is not pretty, but he has a very good disposition and swims as well as the others or even better. I think he will grow up pretty, and perhaps be smaller. He has remained too long in the egg, and therefore his figure is not properly formed"; and then she stroked his neck and smoothed the feathers, saying: "It is a drake, and therefore not of so much consequence. I think he will grow up strong and able to take care of himself."

"The other ducklings are graceful enough," said the old duck. "Now make yourself at home, and if you find an eel's head you can bring it to me."

And so they made themselves comfortable; but the poor duckling who had crept out of his shell last of all and looked so ugly was bitten and pushed and made fun of, not only by the ducks but by all the poultry.

"He is too big," they all said; and the turkey cock, who had been born into the world with spurs and fancied himself really an emperor, puffed himself out like a vessel in full sail and flew at the duckling. He became quite red in the head with passion, so that the poor little thing did not know where to go, and was quite miserable because he was so ugly as to be laughed at by the whole farmyard.

So it went on from day to day; it got worse and worse. The poor duckling was driven about by every one; even his brothers and sisters were unkind to him and would say, "Ah, you ugly creature, I wish the cat would get you" and his mother had been heard to say she wished he had never been born. The ducks pecked him, the chickens beat him, and the girl who fed the poultry pushed him with her feet. So at last he ran away, frightening the little birds in the hedge as he flew over the palings. "They are afraid because I am so ugly," he said. So he flew still farther, until he came out on a large moor inhabited by wild ducks. Here he remained the whole night, feeling very sorrowful.

In the morning, when the wild ducks rose in the air, they stared at their new comrade. "What sort of a duck are you?" they all said, coming round him.

He bowed to them and was as polite as he could be, but he did not reply to their question. "You are exceedingly ugly," said the wild ducks; "but that will not matter if you do not want to marry one of our family."

Poor thing! he had no thoughts of marriage; all he wanted was permission to lie among the rushes and drink some of the water on the moor. After he had been on the moor two days, there came two wild geese, or rather goslings, for they had not been out of the egg long, which accounts for their impertinence. "Listen, friend," said one of them to the duckling; "you are so ugly that we like you very well. Will you go with us and become a bird of passage? Not far from here is another moor, in which there are some wild geese, all of them unmarried. It is a chance for you to get a wife. You may make your fortune, ugly as you are."

"Bang, bang," sounded in the air, and the two wild geese fell dead among the rushes, and the water was tinged with blood. "Bang, bang," echoed far and wide in the distance, and whole flocks of wild geese rose up from the rushes.

The sound continued from every direction, for the sportsmen surrounded the moor, and some were even seated on branches of trees, overlooking the rushes. The blue smoke from the guns rose like clouds over the dark trees, and as it floated away across the water, a number of sporting dogs bounded in among the rushes, which bent beneath them wherever they went. How they terrified the poor duckling! He turned away his head to hide it under his wing, and at the same moment a large, terrible dog passed quite near him. His jaws were open, his tongue hung from his mouth, and his eyes glared fearfully. He thrust his nose close to the duckling, showing his sharp teeth, and then "splash, splash," he went into the water, without touching him.

"Oh," sighed the duckling, "how thankful I am for being so ugly; even a dog will not bite me."

And so he lay quite still, while the shot rattled through the rushes, and gun after gun was fired over him. It was late in the day before all became quiet, but even then the poor young thing did not dare to move. He waited quietly for several hours and then, after looking carefully around him, hastened away from the moor as fast as he could. He ran over field and meadow till a storm arose, and he could hardly struggle against it.

Towards evening he reached a poor little cottage that seemed ready to fall, and only seemed to remain standing because it could not decide on which side to fall first. The storm continued so violent that the duckling could go no farther. He sat down by the cottage, and then he noticed that the door was not quite closed, in consequence of one of the hinges having given way. There was, therefore, a narrow opening near the bottom large enough for him to slip through, which he did very quietly, and got a shelter for the night. Here, in this cottage, lived a woman, a cat, and a hen. The cat, whom his mistress called "My little son," was a great favorite; he could raise his back, and purr, and could even throw out sparks from his fur if it were stroked the wrong way. The hen had very short legs, so she was called "Chickie Short-legs." She laid good eggs, and her mistress loved her as if she had been her own child. In the morning the strange visitor was discovered; the cat began to purr and the hen to cluck.

"What is that noise about?" said the old woman, looking around the room. But her sight was not very good; therefore when she saw the duckling she thought it must be a fat duck that had strayed from home. "Oh, what a prize!" she exclaimed. "I hope it is not a drake, for then I shall have some ducks' eggs. I must wait and see."

So the duckling was allowed to remain on trial for three weeks; but there were no eggs.

Now the cat was the master of the house, and the hen was the mistress; and they always said, "We and the world," for they believed themselves to be half the world, and by far the better half, too. The duckling thought that others might hold a different opinion on the subject, but the hen would not listen to such doubts.

"Can you lay eggs?" she asked. "No." "Then have the goodness to cease talking." "Can you raise your back, or purr, or throw out sparks?" said the cat. "No." "Then you have no right to express an opinion when sensible people are speaking." So the duckling sat in a corner, feeling very low-spirited; but when the sunshine and the fresh air came into the room through the open door, he began to feel such a great longing for a swim that he could not help speaking of it.

"What an absurd idea!" said the hen. "You have nothing else to do; therefore you have foolish fancies. If you could purr or lay eggs, they would pass away."

"But it is so delightful to swim about on the water," said the duckling, "and so refreshing to feel it close over your head while you dive down to the bottom."

"Delightful, indeed! it must be a queer sort of pleasure," said the hen. "Why, you must be crazy! Ask the cat—he is the cleverest animal

I know; ask him how he would like to swim about on the water, or to dive under it, for I will not speak of my own opinion. Ask our mistress, the old woman; there is no one in the world more clever than she is. Do you think she would relish swimming and letting the water close over her head?"

"I see you don't understand me," said the duckling.

"We don't understand you? Who can understand you, I wonder? Do you consider yourself more clever than the cat or the old woman?—I will say nothing of myself. Don't imagine such nonsense, child, and thank your good fortune that you have been so well received here. Are you not in a warm room and in society from which you may learn something? But you are a chatterer, and your company is not very agreeable. Believe me, I speak only for your good. I may tell you unpleasant truths, but that is a proof of my friendship. I advise you, therefore, to lay eggs and learn to purr as quickly as possible."

"I believe I must go out into the world again," said the duckling.

"Yes, do," said the hen. So the duckling left the cottage and soon found water on which it could swim and dive, but he was avoided by all other animals because of his ugly appearance.

Autumn came, and the leaves in the forest turned to orange and gold; then, as winter approached, the wind caught them as they fell and whirled them into the cold air. The clouds, heavy with hail and snowflakes, hung low in the sky, and the raven stood among the reeds, crying, "Croak, croak." It made one shiver with cold to look at him. All this was very sad for the poor little duckling.

One evening, just as the sun was setting amid radiant clouds, there came a large flock of beautiful birds out of the bushes. The duckling had never seen any like them before. They were swans; and they curved their graceful necks, while their soft plumage shone with dazzling whiteness. They uttered a singular cry as they spread their glorious wings and flew away from those cold regions to warmer countries across the sea. They mounted higher and higher in the air, and the ugly little duckling had a strange sensation as he watched them. He whirled himself in the water like a wheel, stretched out his neck towards them, and uttered a cry so strange that it frightened even himself. Could he ever forget those beautiful, happy birds! And when at last they were out of his sight, he dived under the water and rose again almost beside himself with excitement. He knew not the names of these birds nor where they had flown, but he felt towards them as he had never felt towards any other bird in the world.

He was not envious of these beautiful creatures; it never occurred to him to wish to be as lovely as they. Poor ugly creature, how gladly he would have lived even with the ducks, had they only treated him kindly and given him encouragement.

The winter grew colder and colder; he was obliged to swim about on the water to keep it from freezing, but every night the space on which he swam became smaller and smaller. At length it froze so hard that the ice in the water crackled as he moved, and the duckling had to paddle with his legs as well as he could, to keep the space from closing up. He became exhausted at last and lay still and helpless, frozen fast in the ice.

Early in the morning a peasant who was passing by saw what had happened. He broke the ice in pieces with his wooden shoe and carried the duckling home to his wife. The warmth revived the poor little creature; but when the children wanted to play with him, the duckling thought they would do him some harm, so he started up in terror, fluttered into the milk pan, and splashed the milk about the room. Then the woman clapped her hands, which frightened him still more. He flew first into the butter cask, then into the meal tub and out again. What a condition he was in! The woman screamed and struck at him with the tongs; the children laughed and screamed and tumbled over each other in their efforts to catch him, but luckily he escaped. The door stood open; the poor creature could just manage to slip out among the bushes and lie down quite exhausted in the newly fallen snow.

It would be very sad were I to relate all the misery and privations which the poor little duckling endured during the hard winter; but when it had passed he found himself lying one morning in a moor, amongst the rushes. He felt the warm sun shining and heard the lark singing and saw that all around was beautiful spring.

Then the young bird felt that his wings were strong, as he flapped them against his sides and rose high into the air. They bore him onwards until, before he well knew how it had happened, he found himself in a large garden. The apple trees were in full blossom, and the fragrant elders bent their long green branches down to the stream, which wound round a smooth lawn. Everything looked beautiful in the freshness of early spring. From a thicket close by came three beautiful white swans, rustling their feathers and swimming lightly over the smooth water. The duckling saw these lovely birds and felt more strangely unhappy than ever.

"I will fly to these royal birds," he exclaimed, "and they will kill me because, ugly as I am, I dare to approach them. But it does not matter; better be killed by them than pecked by the ducks, beaten by the hens, pushed about by the maiden who feeds the poultry, or starved with hunger in the winter."

Then he flew to the water and swam towards the beautiful swans. The moment they espied the stranger they rushed to meet him with outstretched wings.

"Kill me," said the poor bird and he bent his head down to the surface of the water and awaited death.

But what did he see in the clear stream below? His own image—no longer a dark-gray bird, ugly and disagreeable to look at, but a graceful and beautiful swan.

To be born in a duck's nest in a farmyard is of no consequence to a bird if it is hatched from a swan's egg. He now felt glad at having suffered sorrow and trouble, because it enabled him to enjoy so much better all the pleasure and happiness around him; for the great swans swam round the newcomer and stroked his neck with their beaks, as a welcome.

Into the garden presently came some little children and threw bread and cake into the water.

"See," cried the youngest, "there is a new one"; and the rest were delighted, and ran to their father and mother, dancing and clapping their hands and shouting joyously, "There is another swan come; a new one has arrived."

Then they threw more bread and cake into the water and said, "The new one is the most beautiful of all, he is so young and pretty." And the old swans bowed their heads before him.

Then he felt quite ashamed and hid his head under his wing, for he did not know what to do, he was so happy—yet he was not at all proud. He had been persecuted and despised for his ugliness, and now he heard them say he was the most beautiful of all the birds. Even the elder tree bent down its boughs into the water before him, and the sun shone warm and bright. Then he rustled his feathers, curved his slender neck, and cried joyfully, from the depths of his heart, "I never dreamed of such happiness as this while I was the despised ugly duckling."

PLANT AN INDOOR FLOWER OR HERB GARDEN

Learning about gardening is a great way to cultivate a love for nature in your children, and planting flowers or herbs is a great way to teach them how to nurture and care for the garden as it grows.

WHAT YOU'LL NEED:

First you'll need to decide what you'd like to plant together! These are some of the flowers and herbs that are easily grown indoors:

Flowers: Miniature roses, pansies, impatiens, dwarf sunflowers, nasturtiums, petunias, geraniums, marigolds

Herbs: Basil, parsley, chives, mint, lavender, oregano, rosemary, sage, thyme, tarragon

1. Next, you'll need to find a container to plant your seeds in. A terra cotta pot works well, along with plastic or ceramic pots. But you can be as creative as you'd like. Old mugs, pots and pans, a sand pail, baskets (with a liner, of course), cookie jars, and coffee cans would all make for interesting planters! If you choose an unconventional container that you cannot make drainage holes in, add some rocks (or even marbles) in the bottom to provide drainage for the soil. Make sure there is something underneath your "pot" to catch any extra water.

2. Once you have your container, fill it with potting soil, leaving a few inches at the top. You can buy potting soil that is perfect for indoor planting at any garden center. Don't pack the soil in too tight, just give it a shake and let the soil settle in.

3. Now it's time to plant! Drop the seeds you've chosen on top of the soil, then cover with another ½" layer of earth.

4. Leave them to grow in a sunny window, remembering to water your flowers when the soil feels dry!

Little Bo-Peep

Little Bo-Peep has lost her sheep,
And can't tell where to find them;
Leave them alone, and they'll come home,
Wagging their tails behind them.

Little Bo-Peep fell fast asleep,
And dreamt she heard them bleating;
But when she awoke, she found it a joke,
For still they all were fleeting.

Then up she took her little crook,
Determined for to find them;
She found them indeed, but it made her heart bleed,
For they'd left all their tails behind them!

It happened one day, as Bo-peep did stray
Unto a meadow hard by—
There she espied their tails, side by side,
All hung on a tree to dry.

She heaved a sigh and wiped her eye,
And over the hillocks she raced;
And tried what she could, as a shepherdess should,
That each tail should be properly placed.

MOM'S

APPLE PIE

It turns out that the secret to Mom's Apple Pie is that it's easy to make! After a family trip to the apple orchard, try this recipe—kids will love making a dessert with the apples they just picked. Try preparing with different fruits, as well, such as fresh peaches or pears.

SERVES 8-10

INGREDIENTS

4 apples, peeled, cored, and sliced thinly

½ cup sugar

1 teaspoon vanilla extract

1 teaspoon cinnamon

2 tablespoons trans-fat-free margarine

Pinch of ground nutmeg

1 (12" round) prepared pie crust

1. Preheat oven to 375°F.
2. In a medium saucepan, combine apples, sugar, vanilla, cinnamon, margarine, and nutmeg. Heat on low heat until the apples are soft and the filling is thick, about 20–30 minutes.
3. Fill the crust with apple filling.
4. Bake for 40–45 minutes, until apples are bubbling.

The Four Clever Brothers

BY THE BROTHERS GRIMM

 "**EAR CHILDREN,**" said a poor man to his four sons, "I have nothing to give you; you must go out into the wide world and try your luck. Begin by learning some craft or another, and see how you can get on." So the four brothers took their walking-sticks in their hands, and their little bundles on their shoulders, and after bidding their father goodbye, went all out at the gate together. When they had got on some way they came to four crossways, each leading to a different country. Then the eldest said, "Here we must part; but this day four years we will come back to this spot, and in the meantime each must try what he can do for himself."

So each brother went his way; and as the eldest was hastening on a man met him, and asked him where he was going, and what he wanted. "I am going to try my luck in the world, and should like to begin by learning some art or trade," answered he. "Then," said the man, "go with me, and I will teach you to become the cunningest thief that ever was." "No," said the other, "that is not an honest calling, and what can one look to earn by it in the end but the gallows?" "Oh!" said the man, "you need not fear the gallows; for I will only teach you to steal what will be fair game: I meddle with nothing but what no one else can get or care anything about, and where no one can find you out." So the young man agreed to follow his trade, and he soon showed himself so clever, that nothing could escape him that he had once set his mind upon.

The second brother also met a man, who, when he found out what he was setting out upon, asked him what craft he meant to follow. "I do not know yet," said he. "Then come with me, and be a star-gazer. It is a noble art, for nothing can be hidden from you, when once you understand the stars." The plan pleased him much, and he soon became such a skilful star-gazer, that when he had served out his time, and wanted to leave his master, he gave him a glass, and said, "With this you can see all that is passing in the sky and on earth, and nothing can be hidden from you."

The third brother met a huntsman, who took him with him, and taught him so well all that belonged to hunting, that he became very clever in the craft of the woods; and when he left his master he gave him a bow, and said, "Whatever you shoot at with this bow you will be sure to hit."

The youngest brother likewise met a man who asked him what he wished to do. "Would not you like," said he, "to be a tailor?" "Oh, no!" said the young man; "sitting cross-legged from morning to night, working backwards and forwards with a needle and goose, will never suit me." "Oh!" answered the man, "that is not my sort of tailoring; come with me, and you will learn quite another kind of craft from that." Not knowing what better to do, he came into the plan, and learnt tailoring from the beginning; and when he left his master, he gave him a needle, and said, "You can sew anything with this, be it as soft as an egg or as hard as steel; and the joint will be so fine that no seam will be seen."

After the space of four years, at the time agreed upon, the four brothers met at the four cross-roads; and having welcomed each other, set off towards their father's home, where they told him all that had happened to them, and how each had learned some craft.

Then, one day, as they were sitting before the house under a very high tree, the father said, "I should like to try what each of you can do in this way." So he looked up, and said to the second son, "At the top of this tree there is a chaffinch's nest; tell me how many eggs there are in it." The star-gazer took his glass, looked up, and said, "Five." "Now," said the father to the eldest son, "take away the eggs without letting the bird that is sitting upon them and hatching them know anything of what you are doing." So the cunning thief climbed up the tree, and brought away to his father the five eggs from under the bird; and it never saw or felt what he was doing, but kept sitting on at its ease. Then the father took the eggs, and put one on each corner of the table, and the fifth in the middle, and said to the huntsman, "Cut all the eggs in two pieces at one shot." The huntsman took up his bow, and at one shot struck all the five eggs as his father wished.

"Now comes your turn," said he to the young tailor; "sew the eggs and the young birds in them together again, so neatly that the shot shall have done them no harm." Then the tailor took his needle, and sewed the eggs as he was told; and when he had done, the thief was sent to take them back to the nest, and put them under the bird without its knowing it. Then she went on sitting, and hatched them: and in a few days they crawled out, and had only a little red streak across their necks, where the tailor had sewn them together.

"Well done, sons!" said the old man; "you have made good use of your time, and learnt something worth the knowing; but I am sure I do not know which ought to have the prize. Oh, that a time might soon come for you to turn your skill to some account!"

Not long after this there was a great bustle in the country; for the king's daughter had been carried off by a mighty dragon, and the king mourned over his loss day and night, and made it known that whoever brought her back to him should have her for a wife. Then the four brothers said to each other, "Here is a chance for us; let us try what we can do." And they agreed to see whether they could not set the princess free. "I will soon find out where she is, however," said the star-gazer, as he looked through his glass; and he soon cried out, "I see her afar off, sitting upon a rock in the sea, and I can spy the dragon close by, guarding her." Then he went to the king, and asked for a ship for himself and his brothers; and they sailed together over the sea, till they came to the right place. There they found the princess sitting, as the star-gazer had said, on the rock; and the dragon was lying asleep, with his head upon her lap. "I dare not shoot at him," said the huntsman, "for I should kill the beautiful young lady also." "Then I will try my skill," said the thief, and went and stole her away from under the dragon, so quietly and gently that the beast did not know it, but went on snoring.

Then away they hastened with her full of joy in their boat towards the ship; but soon came the dragon roaring behind them through the air; for he awoke and missed the princess. But when he got over the boat, and wanted to pounce upon them and carry off the princess, the huntsman took up his bow and shot him straight through the heart so that he fell down dead. They were still not safe; for he was such a great beast that in his fall he overset the boat, and they had to swim in the open sea upon a few planks. So the tailor took his needle, and with a few large stitches put some of the planks together; and he sat down upon these, and sailed about and gathered up all pieces of the boat; and then tacked them together so quickly that the boat was soon ready, and they then reached the ship and got home safe.

When they had brought home the princess to her father, there was great rejoicing; and he said to the four brothers, "One of you shall marry her, but you must settle amongst yourselves which it is to be." Then there arose a quarrel between them; and the star-gazer said, "If I had not found the princess out, all your skill would have been of no use; therefore she ought to be mine." "Your seeing her would have been of no use," said the thief, "if I had not taken her away from the dragon; therefore she ought to be mine." "No, she is mine," said the huntsman; "for if I had not killed the dragon, he would, after all, have torn you and the princess into pieces." "And if I had not sewn the boat together again," said the tailor, "you would all have been drowned, therefore she is mine."

Then the king put in a word, and said, "Each of you is right; and as all cannot have the young lady, the best way is for neither of you to have her: for the truth is, there is somebody she likes a great deal better. But to make up for your loss, I will give each of you, as a reward for his skill, half a kingdom." So the brothers agreed that this plan would be much better than either quarrelling or marrying a lady who had no mind to have them. And the king then gave to each half a kingdom, as he had said; and they lived very happily the rest of their days, and took good care of their father; and somebody took better care of the young lady, than to let either the dragon or one of the craftsmen have her again.

*"The sweetest sounds
to mortals given
Are heard in Mother,
Home, and Heaven."*

—WILLIAM GOLDSMITH BROWN

Old Mother Goose

Old Mother Goose
When she wanted to wander,
Would ride through the air
On a very fine gander.

Ride a Cockhorse

Ride a cockhorse to Banbury Cross,
To see a fine lady upon a white horse.
Rings on her fingers, and bells on her toes,
She shall have music wherever she goes.

Rub-A-Dub-Dub

Rub-a-dub-dub
Three men in a tub,
And how do you think they got there?
The butcher, the baker, the candlestick maker,
They all jumped out of a rotten potato,
'Twas enough to make a man stare.

Sneezing

If you sneeze on Monday, you sneeze for danger;
Sneeze on a Tuesday, kiss a stranger;
Sneeze on a Wednesday, sneeze for a letter;
Sneeze on a Thursday, something better.
Sneeze on a Friday, sneeze for sorrow;
Sneeze on a Saturday, joy tomorrow.

Georgie Porgie

Georgie Porgie, pudding and pie,
Kissed the girls and made them cry.
When the boys came out to play,
Georgie Porgie ran away.

Jack and the Beanstalk

JACK SELLS THE COW

NCE UPON A TIME there was a poor widow who lived in a little cottage with her only son Jack.

Jack was a giddy, thoughtless boy, but very kind-hearted and affectionate. There had been a hard winter, and after it the poor woman had suffered from fever and ague. Jack did no work as yet, and by degrees they grew dreadfully poor. The widow saw that there was no means of keeping Jack and herself from starvation but by selling her cow; so one morning she said to her son, "I am too weak to go myself, Jack, so you must take the cow to market for me, and sell her."

Jack liked going to market to sell the cow very much; but as he was on the way, he met a butcher who had some beautiful beans in his hand. Jack stopped to look at them, and the butcher told the boy that they were of great value, and persuaded the silly lad to sell the cow for these beans.

When he brought them home to his mother instead of the money she expected for her nice cow, she was very vexed and shed many tears, scolding Jack for his folly. He was very sorry, and mother and son went to bed very sadly that night; their last hope seemed gone.

At daybreak Jack rose and went out into the garden.

"At least," he thought, "I will sow the wonderful beans. Mother says that they are just common scarlet-runners, and nothing else; but I may as well sow them."

So he took a piece of stick, and made some holes in the ground, and put in the beans.

That day they had very little dinner, and went sadly to bed, knowing that for the next day there would be none and Jack, unable to sleep from grief and vexation, got up at day-dawn and went out into the garden.

What was his amazement to find that the beans had grown up in the night, and climbed up and up till they covered the high cliff that sheltered the cottage, and disappeared above it! The stalks had twined and twisted themselves together till they formed quite a ladder.

"It would be easy to climb it," thought Jack.

And, having thought of the experiment, he at once resolved to carry it out, for Jack was a good climber. However, after his late mistake about the cow, he thought he had better consult his mother first.

WONDERFUL GROWTH OF THE BEANSTALK

So Jack called his mother, and they both gazed in silent wonder at the Beanstalk, which was not only of great height, but was thick enough to bear Jack's weight.

"I wonder where it ends," said Jack to his mother; "I think I will climb up and see."

His mother wished him not to venture up this strange ladder, but Jack coaxed her to give her consent to the attempt, for he was certain there must be something wonderful in the Beanstalk; so at last she yielded to his wishes.

Jack instantly began to climb, and went up and up on the ladder-like bean till everything he had left behind him—the cottage, the village, and even the tall church tower—looked quite little, and still he could not see the top of the Beanstalk.

Jack felt a little tired, and thought for a moment that he would go back again; but he was a very persevering boy, and he knew that the way to succeed in anything is not to give up. So after resting for a moment he went on.

After climbing higher and higher, till he grew afraid to look down for fear he should be giddy, Jack at last reached the top of the Beanstalk, and found himself in a beautiful country, finely wooded, with beautiful meadows covered with sheep. A crystal stream ran through the pastures; not far from the place where he had got off the Beanstalk stood a fine, strong castle.

Jack wondered very much that he had never heard of or seen this castle before; but when he reflected on the subject, he saw that it was as much separated from the village by the perpendicular rock on which it stood as if it were in another land.

While Jack was standing looking at the castle, a very strange-looking woman came out of the wood, and advanced towards him.

She wore a pointed cap of quilted red satin turned up with ermine, her hair streamed loose over her shoulders, and she walked with a staff. Jack took off his cap and made her a bow.

"If you please, ma'am," said he, "is this your house?"

"No," said the old lady. "Listen, and I will tell you the story of that castle.

"Once upon a time there was a noble knight, who lived in this castle, which is on the borders of Fairyland. He had a fair and beloved wife and several lovely children: and as his neighbors, the little people, were very friendly towards him, they bestowed on him many excellent and precious gifts.

"Rumor whispered of these treasures; and a monstrous giant, who lived at no great distance, and who was a very wicked being, resolved to obtain possession of them.

"So he bribed a false servant to let him inside the castle, when the knight was in bed and asleep, and he killed him as he lay. Then he went to the part of the castle which was the nursery, and also killed all the poor little ones he found there.

"Happily for her, the lady was not to be found. She had gone with her infant son, who was only two or three months old, to visit her old nurse, who lived in the valley; and she had been detained all night there by a storm.

"The next morning, as soon as it was light, one of the servants at the castle, who had managed to escape, came to tell the poor lady of the sad fate of her husband and her pretty babes. She could scarcely believe him at first, and was eager at once to go back and share the fate of her dear ones; but the old nurse, with many tears, besought her to remember that she had still a child, and that it was her duty to preserve her life for the sake of the poor innocent.

The lady yielded to this reasoning, and consented to remain at her nurse's house as the best place of concealment; for the servant told her that the giant had vowed, if he could find her, he would kill both her and her baby. Years rolled on. The old nurse died, leaving her cottage and the few articles of furniture it contained to her poor lady, who dwelt in it, working as a peasant for her daily bread. Her spinning-wheel and the milk of a cow, which she had purchased with the little money she had with her, sufficed for the scanty subsistence of herself and her little son. There was a nice little garden attached to the cottage, in which they cultivated peas, beans, and cabbages, and the lady was not ashamed to go out at harvest time, and glean in the fields to supply her little son's wants.

"Jack, that poor lady is your mother. This castle was once your father's, and must again be yours."

Jack uttered a cry of surprise.

"My mother! oh, madam, what ought I to do? My poor father! My dear mother!"

"Your duty requires you to win it back for your mother. But the task is a very difficult one, and full of peril, Jack. Have you courage to undertake it?"

"I fear nothing when I am doing right," said Jack.

"Then," said the lady in the red cap, "you are one of those who slay giants. You must get into the castle, and if possible possess yourself of a hen that lays golden eggs, and a harp that talks. Remember, all the giant possesses is really yours." As she ceased speaking, the lady of the red hat suddenly disappeared, and of course Jack knew she was a fairy.

Jack determined at once to attempt the adventure; so he advanced, and blew the horn which hung at the castle portal. The door was opened in a minute or two by a frightful giantess, with one great eye in the middle of her forehead.

As soon as Jack saw her he turned to run away, but she caught him, and dragged him into the castle.

"Ho, ho!" she laughed terribly. "You didn't expect to see me here, that is clear! No, I shan't let you go again. I am weary of my life. I am so overworked, and I don't see why I should not have a page as well as other ladies. And you shall be my boy. You shall clean the knives, and black the boots, and make the fires, and help me generally when the giant is out. When he is at home I must hide you, for he has eaten up all my pages hitherto, and you would be a dainty morsel, my little lad."

While she spoke she dragged Jack right into the castle. The poor boy was very much frightened, as I am sure you and I would have been in his place. But he remembered that fear disgraces a man; so he struggled to be brave and make the best of things.

"I am quite ready to help you, and do all I can to serve you, madam," he said, "only I beg you will be good enough to hide me from your husband, for I should not like to be eaten at all."

"That's a good boy," said the Giantess, nodding her head; "it is lucky for you that you did not scream out when you saw me, as the other boys who have been here did, for if you had done so my husband would have awakened and have eaten you, as he did them, for breakfast. Come here, child; go into my wardrobe: he never ventures to open *that*; you will be safe there."

And she opened a huge wardrobe which stood in the great hall, and shut him into it. But the keyhole was so large that it admitted plenty of air, and he could see everything that took place through it. By-and-by he heard a heavy tramp on the stairs, like the lumbering along of a great cannon, and then a voice like thunder cried out;

"Fe, fa, fi-fo-fum,

I smell the breath of an Englishman.

Let him be alive or let him be dead,

I'll grind his bones to make my bread."

"Wife," cried the Giant, "there is a man in the castle. Let me have him for breakfast."

"You are grown old and stupid," cried the lady in her loud tones. "It is only a nice fresh steak off an elephant, that I have cooked for you, which you smell. There, sit down and make a good breakfast."

And she placed a huge dish before him of savory steaming meat, which greatly pleased him, and made him forget his idea of an Englishman being in the castle. When he had breakfasted he went out for a walk; and then the Giantess opened the door, and made Jack come out to help her. He helped her all day. She fed him well, and when evening came put him back in the wardrobe.

THE HEN THAT LAYS GOLDEN EGGS

The Giant came in to supper. Jack watched him through the keyhole, and was amazed to see him pick a wolf's bone, and put half a fowl at a time into his capacious mouth.

When the supper was ended he bade his wife bring him his hen that laid the golden eggs.

"It lays as well as it did when it belonged to that paltry knight," he said; "indeed I think the eggs are heavier than ever."

The Giantess went away, and soon returned with a little brown hen, which she placed on the table before her husband. "And now, my dear," she said, "I am going for a walk, if you don't want me any longer."

"Go," said the Giant; "I shall be glad to have a nap by-and-by."

Then he took up the brown hen and said to her:

"Lay!" And she instantly laid a golden egg.

"Lay!" said the Giant again. And she laid another.

"Lay!" he repeated the third time. And again a golden egg lay on the table.

Now Jack was sure this hen was that of which the fairy had spoken.

By-and-by the Giant put the hen down on the floor, and soon after went fast asleep, snoring so loud that it sounded like thunder.

Directly Jack perceived that the Giant was fast asleep, he pushed open the door of the wardrobe and crept out; very softly he stole across the room, and, picking up the hen, made haste to quit the apartment. He knew the way to the kitchen, the door of which he found was left ajar; he opened it, shut and locked it after him, and flew back to the Beanstalk, which he descended as fast as his feet would move.

When his mother saw him enter the house she wept for joy, for she had feared that the fairies had carried him away, or that the Giant had found him. But Jack put the brown hen down before her, and told her how he had been in the Giant's castle, and all his adventures. She was very glad to see the hen, which would make them rich once more.

THE MONEY BAGS

Jack made another journey up the Beanstalk to the Giant's castle one day while his mother had gone to market; but first he dyed his hair and disguised himself. The old woman did not know him again, and dragged him in as she had done before, to help her to do the work; but she heard her husband coming, and hid him in the wardrobe, not thinking that it was the same boy who had stolen the hen. She bade him stay quite still there, or the Giant would eat him.

Then the Giant came in saying:

"Fe, fa, fi-fo-fum,

I smell the breath of an Englishman.

Let him be alive or let him be dead,

I'll grind his bones to make my bread."

"Nonsense!" said the wife, "it is only a roasted bullock that I thought would be a tit-bit for your supper; sit down and I will bring it up at once." The Giant sat down, and soon his wife brought up a roasted bullock on a large dish, and they began their supper. Jack was amazed to see them pick the bones of the bullock as if it had been a lark. As soon as they had finished their meal, the Giantess rose and said:

"Now, my dear, with your leave I am going up to my room to finish the story I am reading. If you want me call for me."

"First," answered the Giant, "bring me my money bags, that I may count my golden pieces before I sleep." The Giantess obeyed. She went and soon returned with two large bags over her shoulders, which she put down by her husband.

"There," she said; "that is all that is left of the knight's money. When you have spent it you must go and take another baron's castle."

"That he shan't, if I can help it," thought Jack.

The Giant, when his wife was gone, took out heaps and heaps of golden pieces, and counted them, and put them in piles, till he was tired of the amusement. Then he swept them all back into their bags, and leaning back in his chair fell fast asleep, snoring so loud that no other sound was audible.

Jack stole softly out of the wardrobe, and taking up the bags of money (which were his very own, because the Giant had stolen them from his father), he ran off, and with great difficulty descending the Beanstalk, laid the bags of gold on his mother's table. She had just returned from town, and was crying at not finding Jack.

"There, mother, I have brought you the gold that my father lost."

"Oh, Jack! you are a very good boy, but I wish you would not risk your precious life in the Giant's castle. Tell me how you came to go there again."

And Jack told her all about it.

Jack's mother was very glad to get the money, but she did not like him to run any risk for her.

But after a time Jack made up his mind to go again to the Giant's castle.

THE TALKING HARP

So he climbed the Beanstalk once more, and blew the horn at the Giant's gate. The Giantess soon opened the door; she was very stupid, and did not know him again, but she stopped a minute before she took him in. She feared another robbery; but Jack's fresh face looked so innocent that she could not resist him, and so she bade him come in, and again hid him away in the wardrobe.

By-and-by the Giant came home, and as soon as he had crossed the threshold he roared out:

"Fe, fa, fi-fo-fum,

I smell the breath of an Englishman.

Let him be alive or let him be dead,

I'll grind his bones to make my bread."

"You stupid old Giant," said his wife, "you only smell a nice sheep, which I have grilled for your dinner."

And the Giant sat down, and his wife brought up a whole sheep for his dinner. When he had eaten it all up, he said:

"Now bring me my harp, and I will have a little music while you take your walk."

The Giantess obeyed, and returned with a beautiful harp. The framework was all sparkling with diamonds and rubies, and the strings were all of gold.

"This is one of the nicest things I took from the knight," said the Giant. "I am very fond of music, and my harp is a faithful servant."

So he drew the harp towards him, and said:

"Play!"

And the harp played a very soft, sad air.

"Play something merrier!" said the Giant.

And the harp played a merry tune.

"Now play me a lullaby," roared the Giant; and the harp played a sweet lullaby, to the sound of which its master fell asleep.

Then Jack stole softly out of the wardrobe, and went into the huge kitchen to see if the Giantess had gone out; he found no one there, so he went to the door and opened it softly, for he thought he could not do so with the harp in his hand.

Then he entered the Giant's room and seized the harp and ran away with it; but as he jumped over the threshold the harp called out:

"Master! Master!"

And the Giant woke up.

With a tremendous roar he sprang from his seat, and in two strides had reached the door.

But Jack was very nimble. He fled like lightning with the harp, talking to it as he went (for he saw it was a fairy), and telling it he was the son of its old master, the knight.

Still the Giant came on so fast that he was quite close to poor Jack, and had stretched out his great hand to catch him. But, luckily, just at that moment he stepped upon a loose stone, stumbled, and fell flat on the ground, where he lay at his full length.

This accident gave Jack time to get on the Beanstalk and hasten down it; but just as he reached their own garden he beheld the Giant descending after him.

"Mother O Mother!" cried Jack, "make haste and give me the ax."

His mother ran to him with a hatchet in her hand, and Jack with one tremendous blow cut through all the Beanstalks except one.

"Now, mother, stand out of the way!" said he.

THE GIANT BREAKS HIS NECK

Jack's mother shrank back, and it was well she did so, for just as the Giant took hold of the last branch of the Beanstalk, Jack cut the stem quite through and darted from the spot.

Down came the Giant with a terrible crash, and as he fell on his head, he broke his neck, and lay dead at the feet of the woman he had so much injured.

Before Jack and his mother had recovered from their alarm and agitation, a beautiful lady stood before them.

"Jack," said she, "you have acted like a brave knight's son, and deserve to have your inheritance restored to you. Dig a grave and bury the Giant, and then go and kill the Giantess."

"But," said Jack, "I could not kill anyone unless I were fighting with him; and I could not draw my sword upon a woman. Moreover, the Giantess was very kind to me."

The Fairy smiled on Jack.

"I am very much pleased with your generous feeling," she said. "Nevertheless, return to the castle, and act as you will find needful."

Jack asked the Fairy if she would show him the way to the castle, as the Beanstalk was now down. She told him that she would drive him there in her chariot, which was drawn by two peacocks. Jack thanked her, and sat down in the chariot with her.

The Fairy drove him a long distance round, till they reached a village which lay at the bottom of the hill. Here they found a number of miserable-looking men assembled. The Fairy stopped her carriage and addressed them:

"My friends," said she, "the cruel giant who oppressed you and ate up all your flocks and herds is dead, and this young gentleman was the means of your being delivered from him, and is the son of your kind old master, the knight."

The men gave a loud cheer at these words, and pressed forward to say that they would serve Jack as faithfully as they had served his father. The Fairy bade them follow her to the castle, and they marched thither in a body, and Jack blew the horn and demanded admittance.

The old Giantess saw them coming from the turret loop-hole. She was very much frightened, for she guessed that something had happened to her husband; and as she came downstairs very fast she caught her foot in her dress, and fell from the top to the bottom and broke her neck.

When the people outside found that the door was not opened to them, they took crowbars and forced the portal. Nobody was to be seen, but on leaving the hall they found the body of the Giantess at the foot of the stairs.

Thus Jack took possession of the castle. The Fairy went and brought his mother to him, with the hen and the harp. He had the Giantess buried, and endeavored as much as lay in his power to do right to those whom the Giant had robbed.

Before her departure for fairyland, the Fairy explained to Jack that she had sent the butcher to meet him with the beans, in order to try what sort of lad he was.

"If you had looked at the gigantic Beanstalk and only stupidly wondered about it," she said, "I should have left you where misfortune had placed you, only restoring her cow to your mother. But you showed an inquiring mind, and great courage and enterprise, therefore you deserve to rise; and when you mounted the Beanstalk you climbed the Ladder of Fortune."

She then took her leave of Jack and his mother.

MOM'S

HOMESTYLE BISCUITS

A family meal is always a little bit better with biscuits. This biscuit dough can be cut into smaller rounds to make mini biscuits, too—have kids help cut the dough. Serve the warm biscuits with butter, honey, jam, sausage patties, or ham for breakfast, or serve them with dinner instead of dinner rolls.

SERVES 8

3 cups all-purpose flour
4½ teaspoons baking powder
1½ teaspoons salt

1 tablespoon sugar
6 tablespoons cold butter
1¼ cups buttermilk

1. Preheat oven to 400°F.
2. Combine flour, baking powder, salt, and sugar in a mixing bowl.
3. Cut butter into small pieces and add to dry ingredients. Mix butter into dry ingredients with a pastry cutter or with your fingers. This mixture should be a bit lumpy so biscuits turn out flaky.
4. Add buttermilk and mix with a wooden spoon to form the dough.
5. Roll dough on a floured board to 1-inch thickness. Cut dough into circles with a 2–3-inch round cookie cutter or a drinking glass. Place rounds on an ungreased baking sheet and bake 12 minutes.

"What good mothers and fathers instinctively feel like doing for their babies is usually best after all."

—BENJAMIN SPOCK

Hansel and Gretel

ADAPTED FROM THE STORY BY THE BROTHERS GRIMM

NCE UPON A TIME there were a little boy and a little girl who lived deep in the forest with their father, a poor wood-cutter, and their cruel stepmother. The little girl was called Gretel, and the boy was named Hansel.

One year, a severe winter settled upon the land and seemed to go on and on without mercy. So it came that the family found itself without enough food to eat. The wicked stepmother told the father that he must take the two children into the forest and leave them behind.

"How can I do that to my poor children?" cried the woodcutter.

"You must!" argued the stepmother. "If you do not, then all four of us shall starve."

Hansel and Gretel were not asleep. When they overheard this conversation, Gretel began to cry.

"Don't worry," Hansel said, "I will find a way to keep us from harm."

The moon shone brightly that night, and Hansel crept downstairs and went outside to collect a pocketful of pebbles that shone brilliantly like the moon.

When morning came, the cruel and wicked stepmother woke the children and gave them each a piece of dry, hard toast for dinner. Then, their father took them into the forest. There, he explained to them that they must remain in the dark woods because there was not enough food at home to feed them. He kissed them and cried as he said good-bye.

As soon as he was gone, Hansel told Gretel about his plan. He had dropped pebbles from out of his pocket, as they walked into the woods with their father. When the moon rose that night, Hansel took his little sister by the hand and they carefully followed the pebbles, which shone like moonbeams. Just as the sun was rising, they arrived back at their father's home.

When their stepmother saw them, she said, "You horrid creatures! We thought you were never coming back!"

Their father cried with joy to see them.

The stepmother was so angry about their return that she plotted their demise once again. One evening, Hansel and Gretel heard their stepmother order their father to leave the children in the forest. That evening, Hansel crept downstairs to collect more pebbles, but found that his stepmother had locked the door to the house. Hansel was resourceful and came up with another plan.

When morning arrived, the wicked stepmother woke the children and gave them each a meager piece of dry toast for dinner. They went with their father into the forest. Along the way, Hansel broke off pieces of bread and dropped the crumbs on the ground to make a trail leading back to their home. Once again, the father kissed the children and said good-bye.

That night, Hansel took his little sister by the hand, and they looked for the white bread crumbs that he had dropped. But they found no bread crumbs, because the creatures of the forest had eaten them all. Hansel, though, felt confident he could find his way out of the forest, even without the bread crumbs to guide their way.

Instead of leading his sister out of the woods, though, Hansel mistakenly led her deeper into the forest. They were very lost and extremely hungry and about to give up all hope, when just ahead in a clearing they saw the strangest little house. It had walls of sweet gingerbread, and a roof of frosted cake. The windows were made of clear sugar and the sidewalk of chocolate.

"I'm going to eat it all!" Hansel said. "I'm going to eat it all!" They both ran to the house and began breaking off pieces, for by now they were very, very hungry.

Then, a soft voice from inside said, "Nibble, nibble, those who roam, who is nibbling on my home?" The children answered, "Only the air, only the air. Blowing here and blowing there."

And they went on eating with gusto!

Suddenly, the door opened, and a woman as old as any they'd ever seen hobbled out. Hansel and Gretel were terribly frightened, but the old woman smiled and said sweetly, "Do come in and stay with me."

She led them inside and fed them pancakes and apples and sugar and nuts and cookies and cakes and puddings. Afterward, she showed them to two beds, where they immediately fell into a deep sleep.

The old woman, who was really a wicked witch, had only pretended to be kind and sweet. While they were sleeping, she seized Hansel and locked him in a little closet behind a grated door. Then she shook Gretel and told her to fetch water and cook something good for Hansel.

"When he is fat," the witch said with glee, "I will eat him!"

Gretel cried, but she was forced to do what the wicked witch commanded. She cooked all the best food in the house for poor Hansel, but she was given nothing to eat but dry bread crusts.

Every morning, the old woman crept to the little closet and told Hansel to stretch out his finger to see if he would soon be fat enough to make a tasty meal. Hansel, however, was very smart. He stretched out a little chicken bone to her. The old woman, who had failing eyesight, thought it was his finger. Week after week went by, and she was astonished that he ate and ate without gaining a single pound.

When a month had passed, and Hansel remained thin, the witch told Gretel she could not wait any longer. "Whether Hansel is fat or thin, tomorrow I will kill him and cook him and eat him!" the witch laughed.

The next morning, the witch woke Gretel and told her that it was time to bake some bread to eat with her meal of Hansel. "The oven is warming and the dough is rising," the witch said. "Creep inside the oven and see if it is hot enough to put the bread in."

Gretel was smart, too, and she knew that the witch intended to lock her up in the oven, bake her, and eat her, too. "I don't understand," Gretel said, "How can I get in?"

"Silly goose," said the old woman, "that door is big enough. Look, I can fit in myself." The old witch crept up and thrust her head into the oven.

Then clever Gretel gave her a big push and shoved her all the way in. She shut the iron door and fastened the bolt. The witch began to howl and scream, but Gretel would not let her out.

Gretel ran like lightning to Hansel, set him free, and cried, "Hansel, we are saved! The old witch is dead."

They hugged and kissed and danced with joy. In the witch's house, they found chests filled with pearls and jewels. They filled their pockets with the treasures.

"But how will we get home?" Gretel asked.

"Don't worry," Hansel said, "I will find a way."

Fortunately for the children, the witch's house was not far from the woodcutter's cabin, and soon they were home. They rushed into the parlor and threw their arms around their father's neck. He had not known one happy hour since he had left his children in the forest. Their stepmother, however, was dead, poisoned by her own cruel spirit. Hansel and Gretel emptied their pockets of pearls and precious stones, and they all lived happily ever after.

MOM'S

GINGERBREAD COOKIES

Use this recipe to make your own gingerbread house, just like the one in "Hansel and Gretel." Or make gingerbread boys and girls, animals, airplanes, or anything you and your kids dream up! Decorate your creations with frosting, jellybeans, gumdrops, sprinkles, or candy. Have fun!

INGREDIENTS

3 cups flour

1 teaspoon baking soda

1 teaspoon ginger

½ teaspoon each of cinnamon, cloves, and nutmeg

1 stick butter or margarine

½ cup sugar

1 egg

½ cup molasses

1 tablespoon vinegar

Your favorite frosting or candies: jellybeans, gumdrops, sprinkles

1. Mix the dry ingredients together.
2. Cream the remaining ingredients.
3. When they are well mixed, add the dry ingredients and mix well. Let the dough chill overnight in a covered container.
4. Roll the dough out on a lightly floured surface until it is ⅛" thick. Then cut it into your favorite shapes.
5. Bake your creations on a cookie sheet at 375°F for about five minutes. Leave a little space between each gingerbread goody on the cookie sheet.
6. When the gingerbread cools, decorate it with frosting or your favorite candies. And enjoy!

"I realized when you look at your mother, you are looking at the purest love you will ever know."

—MITCH ALBOM

MAKE A PAPER BAG VEST

Pretend play is a great way to interact with your kids. But first, make some costumes! Your child can decorate this vest to suit his or her imagination. It can be a cowboy vest, an astronaut suit, or perhaps a police uniform!

WHAT YOU'LL NEED:
1 large brown paper bag
Scissors
Crayons, markers, or paint

1. If the bag has printing on it, gently turn it inside out.
2. Cut a straight line up the middle of the front of the bag.
3. On what was the bottom of the bag, cut a hole large enough for your child's head. Connect the large hole to the slit up the front.
4. Cut armholes on each side, positioned 2"–3" below the fold.
5. Provide different materials for your child to use to decorate the vest.

Little Red Riding Hood

NCE UPON A TIME there lived a little girl who was loved by all for her kind heart. Her grandmother especially loved her and had made her a cape of red wool. The little girl wore the cape all the time, which is why she became known as Red Riding Hood.

One day, her mother asked her to take some chocolate-chip cookies to her ill grandmother who lived across the woods in another village. Off Red Riding Hood went, but it wasn't long before she ran into Mr. Wolf. Being a cruel creature, he had a mind to eat her up. There were men working in the woods, though, and he didn't want to get caught eating the beloved girl, so he came up with another plan.

"Where are you going, my little pretty?" asked the sly wolf.

"I'm going to my grandmother, because she is sick. And I am taking her a basket of chocolate-chip cookies, because she loves them!"

"I see," said the wolf. "Well, I hope your grandmother gets well soon." With that, the wolf ran as fast as he could to the grandmother's house.

When he got there, he knocked at the door. *Toc, toc, toc!*

"Who is there?" asked Grandma.

"Your granddaughter," lied the wolf, imitating Red Riding Hood's voice. "I have brought you some chocolate-chip cookies."

The grandmother invited him in and, before you could say Jack Sprat, he ate the grandmother with his sharp teeth. After he had finished, he climbed into Grandmother's bed and waited for Red Riding Hood.

It wasn't long before she knocked at the door. *Toc, toc, toc!*

"Who is there?" asked the deceitful wolf.

Red Riding Hood, hearing so gruff a voice, was afraid at first. She decided, though, that her grandmother must have a very bad cold indeed to sound so hoarse. So she said, "It is your granddaughter, and I have brought you some chocolate-chip cookies."

The wolf answered her in as soft a voice as he could, "Come on in, sweetie."

And, so she did.

Once inside, the wolf, who was hidden under the covers, said, "Please crawl in with me. I'm very cold."

Sweet little Red Riding Hood agreed and got into bed, but she was frightened by her grandmother's long ears, which came over her nightcap, and by her very long arms, which stuck out the sleeves of her nightie.

So she said, "My, my, what great arms you have got!"

"All the better to hold, my pretty child."

"What long and great ears you have got!"

"All the better to hear, my child."

"What great eyes and long teeth you have got!"

"All the better to see you, and to eat you up."

And as soon as he had said these words, this wicked wolf flew upon poor little Red Riding Hood and ate her up.

"The heart of a mother is a deep abyss at the bottom of which you will always find forgiveness."

—HONORÉ DE BALZAC

As I Was Going To St. Ives

As I was going to St. Ives
I met a man with seven wives.
Every wife had seven sacks,
Every sack had seven cats,
Every cat had seven kits.
Kits, cats, sacks, and wives,
How many were going to St. Ives?

Humpty Dumpty

Humpty Dumpty sat on a wall,
Humpty Dumpty had a great fall;
All the King's horses, and all the King's men
Couldn't put Humpty together again.

There Was a Crooked Man

There was a crooked man, and he went a crooked mile,
He found a crooked sixpence against a crooked stile;
He bought a crooked cat, which caught a crooked mouse,
And they all lived together in a little crooked house.

PLAY "MOTHER, MAY I?"

You'll need at least three players for this game. Choose one player to be "Mother" (or "Father"). You might be an obvious choice, but your children will probably think it's hilarious to "play" Mother!

1. To play, line up your players, or "children," facing "Mother" about ten or so feet away, or on the opposite sides of a room.

2. The players, one by one, ask Mother if they can move forward a certain number of steps (for example, "Mother, may I take five steps forward?"). They can also fill in the blank with different requests, like:

   • "Mother, may I take (#) steps forward?"
   • "Mother, may I take (#) giant steps forward?"
   • "Mother, may I take (#) baby steps forward?"

3. Mother is allowed to respond however she pleases and players must follow the Mother's instructions. If she agrees to the request, she will answer "Yes, _____, you may take one step forward." She may also make another suggestion, answering "No, you may not, but you can _____ instead."

4. Mother doesn't want the children to reach her too quickly, so she may decide to:

   • Reduce the original child's request, allowing a smaller number of steps, for example.
   • Tell a player to take (#) steps backward, run backward for (#) seconds, walk backward until she says "stop," or even tell the player to go back to the starting line.

   The children must obey Mother or they're out of the game.

5. The first of the children to reach Mother wins the game. The winner then becomes the next Mother or Father and a new game begins!

"*A mother's arms are made of tenderness and children sleep soundly in them.*"

—VICTOR HUGO

Wynken, Blynken, and Nod

BY EUGENE FIELD

Wynken, Blynken, and Nod one night
Sailed off in a wooden shoe,
Sailed off on a river of crystal light,
Into a sea of dew.

"Where are you going, and what do you wish?"
The old moon asked the three.
"We have come to fish for the herring fish
That live in the beautiful sea;
Nets of silver and gold have we!"
Said Wynken,
Blynken,
And Nod.

The old moon laughed and sang a song,
As they rocked in the wooden shoe,
And the wind that sped them all night long
Ruffled the waves of dew.

The little stars were the herring fish
That lived in the beautiful sea.
"Now cast your nets wherever you wish—
Never afeard are we";
So cried the stars to the fisherman three:
Wynken,
Blynken,
And Nod.

All night long their nets they threw
To the stars in the twinkling foam—
Then down from the skies came the wooden shoe
Bringing the fisherman home;

'Twas all so pretty a sail it seemed
As if it could not be,
And some folks thought 'twas a dream they'd dreamed
Of sailing that beautiful sea—
But I shall name you the fisherman three:
Wynken,
Blynken,
And Nod.

Wynken and Blynken are two little eyes,
And Nod is a little head,
And the wooden shoe that sailed the skies
Is the wee one's trundle-bed.

So shut your eyes while mother sings
Of wonderful sights that be,
And you shall see the beautiful things
As you rock in the misty sea,
Where the old shoe rocked the fisherman three:
Wynken,
Blynken,
And Nod.

MAKE A PAPER CHAIN

You can sometimes find paper chain kits in the store, but it is cheaper and more fun to make your own. These are a fun way to count down to an exciting event (grandma's visit? The first day of preschool?)—simply tear off a chain "link" per day!

YOU WILL NEED:

Scissors

Lightweight bond paper in various colors

Craft paste sticks

1. Cut out strips of paper 1" wide and 4" long. If your child is adept with safety scissors, he can help you.
2. Show your child how to apply a dab of paste with the paste stick and close each strip to make a link.
3. Help your child attach the links together.
4. When your child has completed a long chain, you hang it up to help brighten the room.

The Little Mermaid

ADAPTED FROM THE STORY BY HANS CHRISTIAN ANDERSEN

NCE UPON A TIME, far out in the deepest part of the ocean, a sea king and his subjects lived. He lived in a magnificent underwater castle with walls of coral, windows of amber, and a roof made of iridescent shells.

The sea king had been a widower for many years, and his old mother kept house for him. She was a very wise woman and very good to the little sea princesses who where her granddaughters. They were six beautiful children, but the youngest was the prettiest of them all with eyes as blue as the sea. Like all the others, she had no feet; her body ended in a fish's tail. She was a strange child, quiet and thoughtful. While her sisters were delighted with the wonderful things that they obtained from shipwrecks, she cared for nothing but the pretty red flowers she grew in the sea garden outside the castle.

She loved to hear about the world above the sea. She made her old grandmother tell her all she knew of the ships and of the towns, the people and the animals.

"When you have reached your fifteenth year," said the grandmother, "you will have permission to rise up out of the sea. Then you will see both forests and towns."

In the following year, one of the sisters would be fifteen. But as each was a year younger than the other, the youngest would have to wait five years before her turn came to rise up from the bottom of the ocean and see Earth. However, each promised to tell the others what she saw on her first visit.

As soon as the eldest was fifteen, she was allowed to rise to the surface of the ocean. When she came back, she had hundreds of things to talk about. But the most beautiful, she said, was to lie in the moonlight and to gaze on a large town nearby, where the lights were twinkling like hundreds of stars.

In another year the second sister received permission to rise to the surface of the water. She rose just as the sun was setting, and this, she said, was the most beautiful sight of all.

The third sister's turn followed. She swam up a broad river that emptied into the sea. On the banks she saw green hills covered with beautiful vines and palaces and castles scattered throughout the forest.

The fourth sister was more timid. She remained in the middle of the sea, but she said it was as beautiful there as nearer the land.

The fifth sister's birthday came in the winter, so when her turn came, she saw what the others had not seen the first time they went up. The sea looked quite green, and large icebergs were floating about.

When the sisters had permission to rise to the surface for the first time, they were each delighted with the new sights. But now, as grownups, they could go when they pleased, and they had become indifferent to it. They wished themselves back again in the water. After a month had passed, they said it was much more beautiful down below and better to be at home.

Their youngest sister, though, thought, "Oh, I wish I were fifteen years old. I know that I shall love the world up there."

At last she reached her fifteenth year. So she said, "Farewell," and rose as lightly as a bubble to the surface. The sea was calm. A large ship lay on the water. There was music and song on board; and, as darkness came on, a hundred colored lanterns were lighted. The little mermaid swam close to the cabin windows; she could look in through the clear glass and see the people inside. Among them was a young prince, the most handsome of all, with intense black eyes; he was sixteen years old.

It was very late, yet the little mermaid could not take her eyes from the ship or from the beautiful prince.

A dreadful storm was approaching. The waves rose as high as mountains. Eventually, the ship's thick planks gave way, and the ship turned over on its side. Water rushed into the ship.

The little mermaid knew that the crew was in danger. At one moment it was so dark that she could not see a single object, but a flash of lightning revealed the whole scene. She could see everyone who had been on board except the prince. When the ship came apart, she had seen him sink into the deep waves; and she was glad, for she thought he would now be with her. Then she remembered that human beings could not live in the water.

She dove into the water to search for him. When she managed to reach the young prince, his beautiful eyes were closed and he would have died without the little mermaid's help. She held his head above the water.

In the morning, the prince's eyes remained closed. The mermaid kissed his forehead and wished that he would live. Presently they came in sight of land. She swam with the handsome prince to the beach and there she laid him in the warm sunshine. Then, the little mermaid swam out from the shore and placed herself between some high rocks that rose out of the water. She covered her head and neck with sea foam, so that her little face wasn't visible and watched to see what would become of the poor prince. She did not wait long before she saw a young girl approach him. Then, the mermaid saw that the prince came to life. She dove sorrowfully into the water, happy that the prince had been saved but sad to be away from him. She returned to her father's castle.

Her sisters asked her what she had seen during her first visit to the surface of the water, but she would tell them nothing.

At length she could bear it no longer and told one of her sisters all about it. Then the others heard the secret, and very soon it became known to two mermaids whose close friend happened to know who the prince was.

"Come, little sister," said the other princesses. They entwined their arms and rose up in a long row to the surface of the water, close by the spot where they knew the prince's palace stood. The little mermaid loved to swim near the shore and watch the prince take his daily walks and make jaunts in his little boat.

The little mermaid was able to think of nothing except the handsome prince. Her grandmother told her that humans found mermaid's tails unattractive and, therefore, the prince would have no interest in her. Desperate for advice, the little mermaid decided to consult an underwater sorceress.

When she arrived at the sorceress's home, the sea witch said, "I know what you want. It is very stupid of you, but you shall have your way and you will be sorry. You want to get rid of your fish's tail and have two legs, so that the young prince may fall in love with you. I will prepare a potion for you. You must swim to land tomorrow before sunrise and drink it. Your tail will then disappear and shrink up into legs. Every step you take will feel as if you were treading upon sharp knives. If you can bear this, I'll help you."

"Yes, I will," said the little mermaid.

"But think again," said the witch, "for once your shape has become like a human, you can no longer be a mermaid."

"I will do it," said the little mermaid.

"But I must be paid also," said the witch, "you must give me your beautiful voice."

"But if you take away my voice," said the little mermaid, "what is left for me?"

"Your beautiful form, your graceful walk, and your expressive eyes."

"All right, then," said the little mermaid.

Then the witch placed her kettle on the fire to prepare the magic potion.

When it was finished, the mermaid took it and swam to the prince's palace. Then the little mermaid drank the magic potion, and it seemed as if a two-edged sword went through her delicate body. Soon she recovered and felt a sharp pain, but before her stood the handsome young prince. She then became aware that her fish's tail was gone and that she had legs but no clothes. She used her long hair to cover herself.

The prince asked her who she was and where she came from, but she could not speak. Every step she took was, as the witch had said it would be, like treading on the points of needles or sharp knives. She followed the prince to the palace and soon was dressed in robes of silk and was the most beautiful creature in the palace. But, because of her deal with the witch, she could not speak.

The prince said she should remain with him. He had a page's dress made for her, so she could go with him on horseback. While at the prince's palace, and when all the household were asleep, she would go and sit on the broad marble steps, for it eased her burning feet to bathe them in the cold seawater.

Once during the night her sisters came up arm-in-arm, singing sorrowfully, as they floated on the water. She beckoned to them, and then they recognized her and told her how much they missed her.

As the days passed, she loved the prince more and more, and he loved her as he would love a little child, but it never crossed his mind to marry her. Yet, according to the laws of the underwater world, unless he married her, she would dissolve into the foam of the sea.

"Do you not love me the best of them all?" the eyes of the little mermaid seemed to say to the prince.

"Yes, you are dear to me," said the prince, "for you have the best heart. You are like a young maiden whom I once saw. I was in a ship that was wrecked and a young maiden found me on the shore and saved my life. She is the only one in the world whom I could love.

"Oh, he doesn't know that I saved his life," thought the little mermaid.

Very soon it was said that the prince must marry, and that the beautiful daughter of a neighboring king would be his wife.

The prince and the little mermaid set sail to meet the woman who was to be his wife. When the princess appeared in front of the palace, her perfect beauty astonished the little mermaid.

"It was you," said the prince, "who saved my life when I was thought to be dead on the beach," and he took his soon-to-be bride into his arms.

The little mermaid kissed his hand and felt as if her heart were already broken. His wedding morning would bring death to her, and she would change into sea foam.

The little mermaid, dressed in silk and gold for the wedding ceremony, held up the bride's train, but her ears heard nothing of the festive music. She thought of the night of death that was coming to her, and of all she had lost in the world.

On the same evening the bride and bridegroom went on board ship. The ship, with swelling sails and a favorable wind, glided away smoothly and lightly over the calm sea. The little mermaid could not help thinking of her first rising out of the sea, when she had seen similar festivities.

She knew this was the last evening she should ever see the prince, for whom she had given up everything. The prince kissed his beautiful bride.

When the party had ended and night fell, she saw her sisters rising out of the flood. They were as pale as herself, but their long beautiful hair waved no more in the wind because it had been cut off.

"We have given our hair to the witch," they said, "so you won't die tonight. She has given us a knife. Before the sun rises you must plunge it into the heart of the prince. When his blood falls upon your feet, they will grow together again and form into a fish's tail, and you will once more be a mermaid."

That night, the little mermaid drew back the curtain of the tent where the prince and his bride were sleeping. She bent down and kissed him. Then she glanced at the sharp knife, and again looked at the prince. She was in his thoughts, and the knife trembled in the hand of the little mermaid. Then she flung it far away from her into the waves. She then threw herself into the sea, and thought her body was dissolving into foam. The sun rose above the waves and the little mermaid did not feel as if she were dying. She saw the bright sun, and all around her floated hundreds of transparent beautiful beings. The little mermaid felt as if she had a body like theirs. She continued to rise higher and higher out of the foam. When the mermaid called out "Where am I going?" she heard this answer:

"Among the daughters of the air. You, poor little mermaid, have tried with your whole heart to do the right thing. You have suffered and endured and raised yourself to the spirit world by your good deeds and kind and happy heart."

PLAY HOPSCOTCH

Hopscotch is a great game for little ones learning to count. Make sure the squares are large enough to fit everyone's feet!

WHAT YOU'LL NEED:

Something to mark the course—you can use sidewalk chalk on asphalt outside, or use masking tape to create a design inside.

1. Design your hopscotch squares as creatively as you'd like and number them, starting with 1. Then find a small object or marker to throw. Outside, a small stone is fitting, and inside, you could use a beanbag, a button, or any other small object.

2. The object of the game is to throw your marker so it lands inside each square without bouncing out or touching the border. If your marker does not land inside the border, your turn is over and play passes to the next person. If it does land inside, hop on one foot through the hopscotch squares in order (unless you reach two squares side by side, in which case you can use both feet, one for each square), hopping over the square with your marker in it. If you hop on or outside the lines or hop in a square out of order, your turn is over.

3. At the last square in your course, turn around on one foot and make your way back through the board. When you come to your marker, stay on one foot, pick it up, and skip over the square it was in until you reach the beginning again. If you reach the beginning without a misstep, then pass the marker on to the next person.

4. To complete the course, landing your marker on each square in order, without losing a turn. The first person to land their marker on each number and complete the course wins the game!

Good Night and Good Morning

BY RICHARD MONCKTON MILNES, LORD HOUGHTON

A fair little girl sat under a tree,
Sewing as long as her eyes could see;
Then smoothed her work, and folded it right,
And said, "Dear work, good night! good night!"

Such a number of rooks came over her head,
Crying, "Caw! Caw!" on their way to bed;
She said, as she watched their curious flight,
"Little black things, good night! good night!"

The horses neighed, and the oxen lowed,
The sheep's "Bleat! bleat!" came over the road;
All seeming to say, with a quiet delight,
"Good little girl, good night! good night!"

She did not say to the sun, "Good night!"
Though she saw him there like a ball of light,
For she knew he had God's time to keep
All over the world, and never could sleep.

The tall pink foxglove bowed his head,
The violets curtsied and went to bed;
And good little Lucy tied up her hair,
And said on her knees her favorite prayer.

And while on her pillow she softly lay,
She knew nothing more till again it was day;
And all things said to the beautiful sun,
"Good morning! good morning! our work is begun!"

SUGAR & SPICE COOKIES

These tasty treats are perfect for any shape cookie cutters you have. Let kids help stamp the shapes, then brush the tops with the egg white.

YIELDS FIVE DOZEN SPICE COOKIES

2½ cups all-purpose flour, sifted
   or stirred before measuring
⅛ teaspoon salt
½ teaspoon cream of tartar
½ teaspoon baking soda
½ teaspoon nutmeg
¼ teaspoon cinnamon

¼ cup shortening
¼ cup butter
1 cup granulated sugar
1 egg
⅓ cup milk
1 egg white, slightly beaten
Granulated sugar

1. Sift together the flour, salt, cream of tartar, baking soda, nutmeg, and cinnamon.
2. In a separate mixing bowl, cream together the shortening and butter with sugar until well mixed and fluffy; carefully add in the egg and milk. When well mixed, slowly add in flour mixture. Chill the dough for two to three hours.
3. When dough has chilled, dust the countertop with flour and roll the dough out to about ¼" thickness; cut out with cookie cutters. Place cookies on cookie sheet and brush the top with the egg white. Sprinkle with sugar and bake at 375°F for about ten minutes or until edges are golden.

Tea and Coffee

Molly, my sister, and I fell out,
And what do you think it was all about?
She loved coffee and I loved tea,
And that was the reason we couldn't agree.

Lucy Locket

Lucy Locket lost her pocket,
Kitty Fisher found it;
There was not a penny in it,
But a ribbon round it.

London Bridge

London Bridge is falling down,
Falling down, falling down;
London Bridge is falling down,
My fair lady.

Build it up with silver and gold,
Silver and gold, silver and gold;
Build it up with silver and gold,
My fair lady.

Silver and gold will be stolen away,
Stolen away, stolen away
Silver and gold will be stolen away,
My fair lady.

Build it up with iron and steel,
Iron and steel, iron and steel
Build it up with iron and steel,
My fair lady.

Iron and steel will bend and bow
Bend and bow, bend and bow
Iron and steel will bend and bow,
My fair lady.

Build it up with wood and clay,
Wood and clay, wood and clay
Build it up with wood and clay,
My fair lady.

Wood and clay will wash away,
Wash away, wash away
Wood and clay will wash away,
My fair lady.

Build it up with stone so strong,
Stone so strong, stone so strong
Stone so strong will last so long,
My fair lady.

To Market, To Market

To market, to market, to buy a fat pig,
Home again, home again, jiggety jig.
To market, to market, to buy a fat hog,
Home again, home again, jiggety jog.
To market, to market, to buy a plum bun,
Home again, home again, market is done.

Simple Simon

Simple Simon met a pieman,
Going to the fair;
Says Simple Simon to the pieman,
"Let me taste your ware."

Says the pieman to Simple Simon,
"Show me first your penny,"
Says Simple Simon to the pieman,
"Indeed, I have not any."

The Elves and the Shoemaker

BY THE GRIMM BROTHERS

HERE WAS ONCE A SHOEMAKER, who worked very hard and was very honest: but still he could not earn enough to live upon; and at last all he had in the world was gone, save just leather enough to make one pair of shoes.

Then he cut his leather out, all ready to make up the next day, meaning to rise early in the morning to his work. His conscience was clear and his heart light amidst all his troubles; so he went peaceably to bed, left all his cares to Heaven, and soon fell asleep. In the morning after he had said his prayers, he sat himself down to his work; when, to his great wonder, there stood the shoes all ready made, upon the table. The good man knew not what to say or think at such an odd thing happening. He looked at the workmanship; there was not one false stitch in the whole job; all was so neat and true, that it was quite a masterpiece.

The same day a customer came in, and the shoes suited him so well that he willingly paid a price higher than usual for them; and the poor shoemaker, with the money, bought leather enough to make two pairs more. In the evening he cut out the work, and went to bed early, that he might get up and begin betimes next day; but he was saved all the trouble, for when he got up in the morning the work was done ready to his hand. Soon in came buyers, who paid him handsomely for his goods, so that he bought leather enough for four pair more. He cut out the work again overnight and found it done in the morning, as before;

and so it went on for some time: what was got ready in the evening was always done by daybreak, and the good man soon became thriving and well off again.

One evening, about Christmas-time, as he and his wife were sitting over the fire chatting together, he said to her, "I should like to sit up and watch tonight, that we may see who it is that comes and does my work for me." The wife liked the thought; so they left a light burning, and hid themselves in a corner of the room, behind a curtain that was hung up there, and watched what would happen.

As soon as it was midnight, there came in two little naked dwarfs; and they sat themselves upon the shoemaker's bench, took up all the work that was cut out, and began to ply with their little fingers, stitching and rapping and tapping away at such a rate, that the shoemaker was all wonder, and could not take his eyes off them. And on they went, till the job was quite done, and the shoes stood ready for use upon the table. This was long before daybreak; and then they bustled away as quick as lightning.

The next day the wife said to the shoemaker, "These little wights have made us rich, and we ought to be thankful to them, and do them a good turn if we can. I am quite sorry to see them run about as they do; and indeed it is not very decent, for they have nothing upon their backs to keep off the cold. I'll tell you what, I will make each of them a shirt, and a coat and waistcoat, and a pair of pantaloons into the bargain; and do you make each of them a little pair of shoes."

The thought pleased the good cobbler very much; and one evening, when all the things were ready, they laid them on the table, instead of the work that they used to cut out, and then went and hid themselves, to watch what the little elves would do.

About midnight in they came, dancing and skipping, hopped round the room, and then went to sit down to their work as usual; but when they saw the clothes lying for them, they laughed and chuckled, and seemed mightily delighted.

Then they dressed themselves in the twinkling of an eye, and danced and capered and sprang about, as merry as could be; till at last they danced out at the door, and away over the green.

The good couple saw them no more; but everything went well with them from that time forward, as long as they lived.

"A mother's arms are more comforting than anyone else's."

—PRINCESS DIANA

Mary, Mary, Quite Contrary

Mary, Mary, quite contrary,
How does your garden grow?
Silver bells and cockle shells,
And pretty maids all in a row.

Hey, Diddle, Diddle

Hey, diddle, diddle!
The cat and the fiddle,
The cow jumped over the moon;
The little dog laughed
To see such sport,
And the dish ran away with the spoon.

Thirty Days Hath September

Thirty days hath September,
April, June, and November;
February has twenty-eight alone,
All the rest have thirty-one,
Excepting leap-year, that's the time
When February's days are twenty-nine.

Pease Porridge Hot

Pease porridge hot,
Pease porridge cold,
Pease porridge in the pot,
Nine days old.
Some like it hot,
Some like it cold,
Some like it in the pot,
Nine days old.

Pat-a-Cake

Pat-a-cake, pat-a-cake, baker's man!
Bake me a cake as fast as you can.
Roll it and pat it, and mark it with B,
And put it in the oven for baby and me.

MOM'S

BUTTERMILK PANCAKES

These basic pancakes can be embellished with many delicious ingredients to make a perfect family breakfast. Blueberries, bananas, chocolate chips, pecans, bacon, green onions, and grated cheese are just a few possible variations. Adding a little cornmeal will give the pancakes some texture.

SERVES 4

1½ cups all-purpose flour

3 tablespoons sugar

1½ teaspoons baking powder

½ teaspoon baking soda

½ teaspoon salt

2 eggs

3 tablespoons butter, melted

1½ cups buttermilk

1. Combine flour, sugar, baking powder, baking soda, and salt in a large bowl, using a whisk.
2. Combine eggs, melted butter, and buttermilk in another bowl with whisk.
3. Add just enough vegetable oil to a frying pan to coat the bottom. If you're using a griddle that isn't nonstick, lightly oil it to prevent pancakes from sticking. Heat pan or griddle over medium heat.
4. Stir egg mixture into the flour mixture until combined, but don't overmix.
5. Pour about ⅛ cup batter onto hot, oiled griddle or pan for each pancake. Flip pancake when bubbles have formed and started to pop on one side. Cook on other side for a minute or two.
6. Serve hot with butter and syrup or fresh fruit, whipped cream, and powdered sugar.

Pinocchio

ADAPTED FROM THE STORY BY CARLO COLLODI

 NCE UPON A TIME a poor carpenter picked up a piece of wood while fixing a table. When he began to chisel it, the wood started to moan. This frightened the carpenter, and he decided to get rid of it at once. So he gave it to his friend, Geppetto, who wanted to make a puppet.

Geppetto, a cobbler, took the wood home, thinking about the name he would give his puppet. "I'll call him Pinocchio," he told himself. "It's a lucky name."

Back at his home, Geppetto started to carve the wood. Suddenly a voice squealed, "Oh! That hurt!"

Geppetto was astonished to find that the wood was alive. Excited, he carved a head, hair, and eyes, which immediately stared right at the cobbler. But the second Geppetto carved out the nose, it grew longer and longer. No matter how often the cobbler cut it down to size, it just stayed a long nose.

When he finished carving the puppet, Geppetto taught him to walk. But the minute Pinocchio stood upright; he opened the door and ran into the street. Luckily, a policeman saw Pinocchio running from the cobbler. He grabbed the runaway and handed him over to his father.

Pinocchio apologized for running away, and Geppetto forgave his son. The cobbler made Pinocchio a suit out of colorful paper, a pair of tree-bark shoes, and a soft felt hat with a big feather. The puppet hugged his father.

"I'd like to go to school," he said, "to become clever and help you when you're old!"

"I'm very grateful," Geppetto replied, "but we haven't enough money to buy you even the first reading book!" Pinocchio looked sad, then Geppetto suddenly stood and went out of the house. Soon he returned carrying a first reading book, a little worn but still perfectly usable.

It was snowing outside. "Where's your coat, Father?"

"I sold it."

"Why did you sell it?"

"It kept me too warm!"

Pinocchio threw his arms round Geppetto's neck and kissed the kindly old man.

The next day, Pinocchio started toward school but was distracted when he heard the sound of a brass band. He ended up in a crowded square where people were clustering round a booth.

"What's that?" he asked a boy.

"Can't you read? It's the Great Puppet Show!"

"How much do you pay to go inside?"

"Fourpence."

"Who'll give me fourpence for this brand-new book?" Pinocchio cried. A nearby junk seller bought the reading book, and Pinocchio hurried into the booth. Once inside the booth, Pinocchio knew he had made a mistake selling the book Geppetto had bought for him. He decided to return to his home and apologize to Geppetto.

Pinocchio sadly trudged home and told Geppetto that a bully had stolen his book. But as he spoke, something strange happened: His nose started to grow. And as he continued to insist the book had been stolen, his nose grew and grew.

"What is happening?" asked an alarmed Pinocchio.

"You're not telling the truth, Pinocchio," answered Geppetto. "When you lie, your nose grows. If you tell me the truth, your nose will return to its normal size."

So, Pinocchio told Geppetto what had happened to the book and his nose shrunk to its normal (but still rather large!) size. After scolding the puppet for selling the book, Geppetto forgave him and sent Pinocchio off to school. But someone else was about to cross his path and lead him astray. This time, it was Carlo, an extremely lazy boy.

"Why don't you come to Toyland with me?" he said. "Nobody ever studies there and you can play all day long!"

"Does such a place really exist?" asked Pinocchio in amazement.

"The wagon comes by this evening to take me there," said Carlo. "Would you like to come?"

Forgetting all his promises to his father, Pinocchio was again heading for trouble. Midnight struck, and the wagon arrived to pick up the two friends, along with some other lads who could hardly wait to reach Toyland.

Twelve pairs of donkeys pulled the wagon, and they were all shod with white leather boots. The boys clambered into the wagon. Pinocchio, the most excited of them all, jumped onto a donkey. Toyland was just as Carlo had described it: The boys all had fun and there was no school.

One day, however, Pinocchio awoke to a rather nasty surprise. When he raised a hand to his head, he found he had sprouted a long pair of hairy ears, in place of the sketchy ears that Geppetto had never got around to finishing. The next day, they had grown longer than ever. Pinocchio pulled on a large cotton cap and went off to search for Carlo. He too was wearing a hat, pulled right down to his nose. With the same thought in their heads, the boys stared at each other. Then snatching off their hats, they began to laugh at the funny sight of the long hairy ears. But as they screamed with laughter, Carlo suddenly went pale and began to stagger. "Pinocchio, help! Help!" But Pinocchio himself was stumbling about, and he burst into tears. For their faces were growing into the shape of a donkey's head, and they felt themselves go down on all fours.

Pinocchio and Carlo were turning into a pair of donkeys. And they started to bray loudly. When the Toyland wagon driver heard the braying of his new donkeys, he rubbed his hands in glee. "There are two fine new donkeys to take to market. I'll get at least four gold pieces for them!" This was the fate that awaited naughty little boys who skipped school. Carlo was sold to a farmer. A circus man bought Pinocchio, and he had to learn circus tricks. One day, as he was jumping through the hoop, he stumbled and went lame.

The circus man called the stable boy. "A lame donkey is no use to me," he said. "Take it to market and get rid of it at any price!" But nobody wanted to buy a useless donkey. Then along came a little man who said, "I'll take it for the skin. It will make a good drum for the village band."

And so, for a few pennies, Pinocchio was purchased. His new owner led him to the edge of the sea, tied a large stone to his neck, and a long rope round his legs, and pushed him into the water. Clutching the end of the rope, the man sat down to wait for Pinocchio to drown. Pinocchio struggled for breath at the bottom of the sea. In a flash, he remembered all the bother he had given Geppetto and all his broken promises, too, and he called on a fairy to help him.

A fairy heard Pinocchio's call and sent a school of big fish. They ate away all the donkey flesh, leaving the wooden Pinocchio. Just then, as the fish stopped nibbling, Pinocchio felt himself hauled out of the water. And the man gasped in astonishment at the living puppet, which appeared in place of the dead donkey. Pinocchio told the man the whole story and dived into the sea. Thankful to be a wooden puppet again, Pinocchio swam happily out to sea and was soon just a dot on the horizon.

But his adventures were far from over. Out of the water behind him loomed a shark with huge teeth! Pinocchio tried to swim away as fast as he could, but the shark only glided closer. Then the puppet tried to escape by going in the other direction, but it was in vain. He could never escape the shark and was soon swallowed by it. When Pinocchio came to his senses, he was in darkness. Suddenly, he noticed a pale light and, as he crept toward it, he saw it was a flame in the distance. On he went.

"Father! It can't be you!"

"Pinocchio! Son! It really is you."

Weeping for joy, they hugged each other and, between sobs, told their adventures. Geppetto told him how he came to be in the shark's stomach. "I was looking for you everywhere. When I couldn't find you on dry land, I made a boat to search for you on the sea. But the boat capsized in a storm, and then the shark ate me."

"Well, we're still alive!" remarked Pinocchio. "We must get out of here!"

The pair started to climb up the shark's stomach, using a candle to light their way. This shark happened to sleep with its mouth open, so they quietly hurried out while it was napping.

At long last, Pinocchio and Geppetto reached home. Geppetto was so ill from his adventures that he was near death. Pinocchio took care of him and held him gently until he recovered. He went to work for a nearby farmer to earn money to buy food for his father.

One night, in a wonderful dream, the fairy appeared to reward Pinocchio for this kindness. When the puppet looked in the mirror next morning, he found he had turned into a real boy. Geppetto hugged him happily.

"Where's the wooden Pinocchio?" the boy asked.

"There!" exclaimed Geppetto, pointing at him. "You've shown you're a real boy with a real kind, giving heart."

MAKE YOUR OWN PINOCCHIO

Although Geppetto's Pinocchio was carved from wood, you can make a Pinocchio (or any other fairy tale character) sock puppet from simple materials.

WHAT YOU'LL NEED:

A sock

Scissors

Felt for the mouth

Needle and thread

A Styrofoam ball to fit inside the toe of the sock

Ribbons, fabrics, buttons, beads, yarn, papers for decorating your puppet

1. Cut a small slit in the heel of the sock, and then turn the sock inside out.
2. Cut a circle of felt to sew into the slit for the mouth. Stitch the felt in place.
3. Turn the sock right side out. Place the Styrofoam ball in the toe of the sock for the head.
4. Now, it's up to you to decorate your puppet. For Pinocchio, you might like to make a little felt hat with a feather, or use paper to form a cone for his nose. Maybe you'd like to make a princess puppet. Cover your socks with sequins to make a princess's dress, or cut gold paper or tin foil to make a glittering crown.

MOM'S

CHEESE PIZZA

Kids love topping their own pizzas. Give them diced or sliced vegetables so they can arrange patterns or faces. Coarsely grate mozzarella and Parmesan cheese just before topping pizzas for best flavor.

MAKES 2 (12") PIZZAS

INGREDIENTS

Dough for 2 (12") pizzas

2 tablespoons cornmeal or
   1 tablespoon olive oil

1½ cups tomato sauce

1 cup shredded Parmesan cheese

3 cups shredded mozzarella
   cheese

Toppings, if desired

1. Roll or press pizza dough into 2 (12") circles, slightly thicker at the edges than in the center. If using pizza pans, sprinkle the bottom with cornmeal or coat with olive oil and place dough in pan. If using a pizza stone, sprinkle with cornmeal and place stone in oven. Preheat oven to 400°F.

2. Spread ¾ cup sauce in the center of each pizza, leaving at least 1" around the edges bare.

3. Sprinkle ½ cup Parmesan over the sauce on each pizza. Distribute 1½ cups mozzarella evenly over each pizza, just covering the sauce. Add toppings, if using.

4. If using a hot stone or tiles, use a well-floured pizza peel to carefully lift one pizza from preparation surface and place on stone. If using pizza pans, place first pizza in the center of the oven. Bake for 15–20 minutes or until the crust is lightly browned and cheese is melted.

5. Remove pizza from oven carefully (use peel if baking with a stone). Set aside to rest briefly before slicing. Repeat baking process with second pie.

"No language can express the power, and beauty, and heroism, and majesty of a mother's love. It shrinks not where man cowers, and grows stronger where man faints, and over wastes of worldly fortunes sends the radiance of its quenchless fidelity like a star."

—EDWIN HUBBELL CHAPIN

A-Tisket, A-Tasket

A-tisket, a-tasket,
A green and yellow basket,
I wrote a letter to my love,
And on the way, I dropped it.

I dropped it, I dropped it,
And on the way I dropped it.
A little boy picked it up
And put it in his pocket.

Rain, Rain

Rain, rain, go away,
Come again another day;
Little Johnny wants to play.

Polly Put the Kettle On

Polly, put the kettle on,
Polly, put the kettle on,
Polly, put the kettle on,
We'll all have tea.

Sukey, take it off again,
Sukey, take it off again,
Sukey, take it off again,
They've all gone away.

The Emperor's New Clothes

ADAPTED FROM THE STORY BY HANS CHRISTIAN ANDERSEN

 NCE UPON A TIME there lived a rather vain emperor whose only care in life was to dress in fancy clothes. He spent hours every day looking through his vast wardrobe, changing his royal garments almost every hour and showing them off to the people in his kingdom. In fact, it was difficult for him to think about anything other than what to wear next.

Word of the emperor's vain habits soon spread throughout the land. As the news traveled, two schemers who had heard of the emperor's desire for the latest clothing fashions decided to take advantage of the situation. They introduced themselves at the gates of the palace with a grand plan in mind.

"We are two very good tailors. After many years of research, we have invented an extraordinary method to weave a cloth so light and fine that it looks invisible. As a matter of fact, it is invisible to anyone too stupid and incompetent to appreciate its quality."

The chief of the guards heard the schemers' strange story and sent for the court chamberlain. The chamberlain notified the prime minister, who ran to the emperor and disclosed the incredible news.

The emperor's curiosity and his desire for up-to-the-minute fashions got the better of him, and he decided to see the two men.

"Besides being so light and fine, Your Highness, this cloth will be woven in colors and designs created especially for you."

The emperor gave the two men a large bag of gold coins in exchange for their promise to begin working on the fabric immediately. "Just tell us what you need to get started and we'll give it to you," he told them.

The two scoundrels asked for a loom, silk, and gold thread. Then they pretended to begin working. The emperor thought he had spent his money quite well for he would gain in two ways. In addition to getting a new extraordinary suit, he would discover which of his subjects were ignorant and incompetent. A few days later, he called in the old and wise prime minister, who was considered by everyone to be a man with common sense.

"Go and see how the work is proceeding," the Emperor told him, "and come back to let me know."

The two scoundrels welcomed the prime minister. "We're almost finished, but we need a lot more gold thread. Here, Excellency! Admire the colors, feel the softness!"

The old man bent over the loom and tried to see the fabric that was not there. He felt cold sweat on his forehead. "I can't see anything," he thought. "If I see nothing, the emperor will think I am incompetent." If he admitted that he didn't see anything, he would be discharged from his office. "What a marvelous fabric," he said. "I'll certainly tell the emperor."

The two scoundrels rubbed their hands gleefully. Finally, the emperor received the announcement that the two tailors had come to take all the measurements needed to make his new suit.

"Come in," the emperor ordered. Even as they bowed, the two scoundrels pretended to be holding an enormous bolt of fabric.

"Here it is, Your Highness, the result of our labor," the scoundrels said. "We have worked night and day, but at last the most beautiful fabric in the world is ready for you. Look at the colors and feel how fine it is."

Of course, the emperor did not see any colors and could not feel any cloth between his fingers. He panicked; he felt like fainting. But luckily the throne was right behind him, so he sat down. But when he realized that no one would know that he did not see the fabric, he felt better. Nobody would find out he was stupid and incompetent. Now the emperor didn't know that everybody else around him thought and did the very same thing.

The scheme continued just as the two scoundrels had hoped. Once they had taken the measurements, the two began cutting the air with scissors while sewing with their needles an invisible cloth.

"Your Highness, you'll have to take off your clothes to try on your new ones." The two scoundrels draped the new clothes on him and then held up a mirror.

The emperor was embarrassed, but since none of the bystanders seemed to notice that he had nothing on, he felt relieved. "Yes, this is a beautiful suit, and it looks very good on me," the emperor said, trying to look comfortable. "You've done a fine job."

"Your Majesty," the prime minister said, "we have a request for you. The people have found out about this extraordinary fabric, and they are anxious to see you in your new suit."

The emperor was doubtful about showing himself naked to the people, but then he abandoned his fears. After all, only the ignorant and the incompetent wouldn't be able to see his new suit.

"All right," he said. "I will grant the people the delight of seeing my new clothes."

He summoned his carriage and the ceremonial parade was formed. A group of dignitaries walked at the very front of the procession and anxiously scrutinized the faces of the people in the street.

All the people had gathered in the main square, pushing and shoving to get a better look at the famous new clothes. Applause welcomed the regal parade. Everyone wanted to know how stupid or incompetent his or her neighbor was. But as the emperor passed, strange murmurs rose from the crowd that were loud enough for everyone to hear: "Look at the emperor's new clothes. They're beautiful!" "What a marvelous train!" "And look at the magnificent colors! The colors of that beautiful fabric! I have never seen anything like it in my life."

The people all tried to conceal their disappointment at not being able to see the clothes. But since no one was willing to admit his or her own stupidity and incompetence, they all behaved as the two scoundrels had predicted.

A child, however, who had no important job and could only see things as his eyes showed them to him, went up to the carriage. "The emperor is naked," he said.

"Fool!" his father said. "Don't talk nonsense!" He grabbed his child and took him away.

But the boy's remark, which had been heard by the others, was repeated over and over until everyone cried: "The boy is right! The emperor is naked! It's true!"

The emperor realized that the people were right, but he certainly could not admit it. He though it wiser to continue the procession under the illusion that anyone who couldn't see his clothes was either stupid or incompetent. And he stood stiffly on his carriage, while behind him a page held his imaginary royal cloak.

The Farmer in the Dell

The farmer in the dell,
The farmer in the dell,
Hi-ho, the derry-o,
The farmer in the dell.

The farmer takes a wife,
The farmer takes a wife,
Hi-ho, the derry-o,
The farmer takes a wife.

The wife takes a child,
The wife takes a child,
Hi-ho, the derry-o,
The wife takes a child.

The child takes a nurse,
The child takes a nurse,
Hi-ho, the derry-o,
The child takes a nurse.

The nurse takes the cow,
The nurse takes the cow,
Hi-ho, the derry-o,
The nurse takes the cow.

The cow takes a dog,
The cow takes a dog,
Hi-ho, the derry-o,
The cow takes a dog.

The dog takes a cat,
The dog takes a cat,
Hi-ho, the derry-o,
The dog takes a cat.

The cat takes a rat,
The cat takes a rat,
Hi-ho, the derry-o,
The cat takes a rat.

The rat takes the cheese,
The rat takes the cheese,
Hi-ho, the derry-o,
The rat takes the cheese

The cheese stands alone,
The cheese stands alone,
Hi-ho, the derry-o,
The cheese stands alone.

"*Motherhood has a very humanizing effect. Everything gets reduced to essentials.*"

—MERYL STREEP

Little Snow-White
(Snow White and the Seven Dwarfs)

BY THE BROTHERS GRIMM

I T WAS IN THE MIDDLE OF WINTER, when the broad flakes of snow were falling around, that a certain queen sat working at her window, the frame of which was made of fine black ebony; and, as she was looking out upon the snow, she pricked her finger, and three drops of blood fell upon it. Then she gazed thoughtfully down on the red drops which sprinkled the white snow and said, "Would that my little daughter may be as white as that snow, as red as the blood, and as black as the ebony window-frame!" And so the little girl grew up; her skin was as white as snow, her cheeks as rosy as blood, and her hair as black as ebony; and she was called Snow White.

But this queen died; and the king soon married another wife, who was very beautiful, but so proud that she could not bear to think that any one could surpass her. She had a magical looking-glass, to which she used to go and gaze upon herself in it, and say—

"Tell me, glass, tell me true!
Of all the ladies in the land,
Who is fairest? tell me who?"

And the glass answered, "Thou, Queen, art fairest in the land."

But Snow-White grew more and more beautiful; and when she was seven years old, she was as bright as the day, and fairer than the queen herself. Then the glass one day answered the queen, when she went to consult it as usual—

"Thou, Queen, may'st fair and beauteous be,
But Snow-White is lovelier far than thee."

When the queen heard this she turned pale with rage and envy; and calling to one of her servants said, "Take Snow-White away into the wide wood, that I may never see her more." Then the servant led the little girl away; but his heart melted when she begged him to spare her life, and he said, "I will not hurt thee, thou pretty child." So he left her there alone; and though he thought it most likely that the wild beasts would tear her to pieces, he felt as if a great weight were taken off his heart when he had made up his mind not to kill her, but leave her to her fate.

Then poor Snow-White wandered along through the wood in great fear; and the wild beasts roared around, but none did her any harm. In the evening she came to a little cottage, and went in there to rest, for her weary feet would carry her no further. Everything was spruce and neat in the cottage: on the table was spread a white cloth, and there were seven little plates with seven little loaves and seven little glasses with wine in them; and knives and forks laid in order, and by the wall stood seven little beds. Then, as she was exceedingly hungry, she picked a little piece off each loaf, and drank a very little wine out of each glass; and after that she thought she would lie down and rest. So she tried all the little beds; and one was too long, and another was too short, till, at last, the seventh suited her; and there she laid herself down and went to sleep. Presently in came the masters of the cottage, who were seven little dwarfs that lived among the mountains, and dug and searched about for gold. They lighted up their seven lamps, and saw directly that all was not right. The first said, "Who has been sitting on my stool?" The second, "Who has been eating off my plate?" The third, "Who has been picking at my bread?" The fourth, "Who has been meddling with my spoon?" The fifth, "Who has been handling my fork?" The sixth,

"Who has been cutting with my knife?" The seventh, "Who has been drinking my wine?" Then the first looked around and said, "Who has been lying on my bed?" And the rest came running to him, and every one cried out that somebody had been upon his bed. But the seventh saw Snow-White, and called upon his brethren to come and look at her; and they cried out with wonder and astonishment, and brought their lamps and gazing upon her, they said, "Good heavens! what a lovely child she is!" And they were delighted to see her, and took care not to waken her; and the seventh dwarf slept an hour with each of the other dwarfs in turn, till the night was gone.

In the morning Snow-White told them all her story, and they pitied her, and said if she would keep all things in order, and cook and wash, and knit and spin for them, she might stay where she was, and they would take good care of her. Then they went out all day long to their work, seeking for gold and silver in the mountains; and Snow-White remained at home; and they warned her, saying, "The queen will soon find out where you are, so take care and let no one in." But the queen, now that she thought Snow-White was dead, believed that she was certainly the handsomest lady in the land; so she went to her glass and said—

"Tell me, glass, tell me true!
Of all the ladies in the land,
Who is fairest? tell me who?"

And the glass answered—

"Thou, Queen, thou are fairest in all this land;
But over the Hills, in the greenwood shade,
Where the seven dwarfs their dwelling have made,
There Snow-White is hiding; and she
Is lovelier far, O Queen, than thee."

Then the queen was very much alarmed; for she knew that the glass always spoke the truth, and she was sure that the servant had betrayed her. And as she could not bear to think that any one lived who was more beautiful than she was, she disguised herself as an old pedlar woman and went her way over the hills to the place where the dwarfs dwelt. Then she knocked at the door and cried, "Fine wares to sell!" Snow-White looked out of the window, and said, "Good day, good woman; what have you to sell?" "Good wares, fine wares," replied she; "laces and bobbins of all colors." "I will let the old lady in; she seems to be a very good sort of a body," thought Snow-White; so she ran down, and unbolted the door. "Bless me!" said the woman, "how badly your stays are laced. Let me lace them up with one of my nice new laces." Snow-White did not dream of any mischief; so she stood up before the old woman who set to work so nimbly, and pulled the lace so tightly that Snow-White lost her breath, and fell down as if she were dead. "There's an end of all thy beauty," said the spiteful queen, and went away home.

In the evening the seven dwarfs returned; and I need not say how grieved they were to see their faithful Snow-White stretched upon the ground motionless, as if she were quite dead. However, they lifted her up, and when they found what was the matter, they cut the lace; and in a little time she began to breathe, and soon came to herself again. Then they said, "The old woman was the queen; take care another time, and let no one in when we are away."

When the queen got home, she went to her glass, and spoke to it, but to her surprise it replied in the same words as before.

Then the blood ran cold in her heart with spite and malice to hear that Snow-White still lived; and she dressed herself up again in a disguise, but very different from the one she wore before, and took with her a poisoned comb. When she reached the dwarfs' cottage, she knocked at the door, and cried, "Fine wares to sell!" but Snow-White said, "I dare not let any one in." Then the queen said, "Only look at my beautiful combs"; and gave her the poisoned one. And it looked so pretty that the little girl took it up and put it into her hair to try it; but the moment it touched her head the poison was so powerful that she fell down senseless. "There you may lie," said the queen, and went her way. But by good luck the dwarfs returned very early that evening; and when they saw Snow-White lying on the ground, they thought what had happened, and soon found the poisoned comb. And when they took it away, she recovered, and told them all that had passed; and they warned her once more not to open the door to any one.

Meantime the queen went home to her glass, and trembled with rage when she received exactly the same answer as before; and she said, "Snow-White shall die, if it costs me my life." So she went secretly into a chamber, and prepared a poisoned apple: the outside looked very rosy and tempting, but whosoever tasted it was sure to die. Then she dressed herself up as a peasant's wife, and traveled over the hills to the dwarfs' cottage, and knocked at the door; but Snow-White put her head out of the window, and said, "I dare not let any one in, for the dwarfs have told me not to." "Do as you please," said the old woman, "but at any rate take this pretty apple; I will make you a present of it." "No," said Snow-White, "I dare not take it." "You silly girl!" answered the other, "what are you afraid of? do you think it is poisoned? Come! do you eat one part, and I will eat the other." Now the apple was so prepared that one side was good, though the other side was poisoned. Then Snow-White was very much tempted to taste, for the apple looked exceedingly nice; and when she saw the old woman eat, she could refrain no longer. But she had scarcely put the piece into her mouth when she fell down dead upon the ground. "This time nothing will save thee," said the queen; and she went home to her glass, and at last it said—"Thou, Queen, art the fairest of all the fair." And then her envious heart was glad, and as happy as such a heart could be.

When evening came, and the dwarfs returned home, they found Snow-White lying on the ground; no breath passed her lips, and they were afraid that she was quite dead. They lifted her up, and combed her hair, and washed her face with wine and water; but all was in vain. So they laid her down upon a bier, and all seven watched and bewailed her three whole days; and then they proposed to bury her; but her cheeks were still rosy, and her face looked just as it did while she was alive; so they said, "We will never bury her in the cold ground." And they made a coffin of glass so that they might still look at her, and wrote her name upon it in golden letters, and that she was a king's daughter. Then the coffin was placed upon the hill, and one of the dwarfs always sat by it and watched. And the birds of the air came, too, and bemoaned Snow-White. First of all came an owl, and then a raven, but at last came a dove.

And thus Snow-White lay for a long, long time, and still only looked as though she were asleep; for she was even now as white as snow, and as red as blood, and as black as ebony. At last a prince came and called at the dwarfs' house; and he saw Snow-White and read what was written in golden letters. Then he offered the dwarfs money, and earnestly prayed them to let him take her away; but they said, "We will not part with her for all the gold in the world." At last, however, they had pity on him, and gave him the coffin; but the moment he lifted it up to carry it home with him, the piece of apple fell from between her lips, and Snow-White awoke, and exclaimed, "Where am I!" And the prince answered, "Thou art safe with me." Then he told her all that had happened, and said, "I love you better than all the world; come with me to my father's palace, and you shall be my wife." Snow-White consented, and went home with the prince; and everything was prepared with great pomp and splendor for their wedding.

To the feast was invited, among the rest, Snow-White's old enemy, the queen; and as she was dressing herself in fine, rich clothes, she looked in the glass and said,

"Tell me, glass, tell me true!
Of all the ladies in the land,
Who is fairest? tell me who?"

And the glass answered,

"Thou, lady, art the loveliest here, I ween;
But lovelier far is the new-made queen."

When she heard this, the queen started with rage; but her envy and curiosity were so great, that she could not help setting out to see the bride. And when she arrived, and saw that it was no other than Snow-White, whom she thought had been dead a long while, she choked with passion, and fell ill and died; but Snow-White and the prince lived and reigned happily over that land, many, many years.

MOM'S

BLUEBERRY MUFFINS

When everyone's up early, try making a batch of these muffins and eating them warm out of the oven. This basic muffin recipe can be used to make different muffins by substituting blackberries, raspberries, cranberries, chocolate chips, peaches, or pecans for the blueberries. Add orange zest to the cranberries, lemon zest to the blueberries, or chopped hazelnuts to the chocolate chips for more variety.

SERVES 12

INGREDIENTS

2 cups all-purpose flour

⅔ cup sugar

1 tablespoon baking powder

½ teaspoon salt

2 eggs

1 cup milk

6 tablespoons butter, melted

1 teaspoon vanilla extract

1½ cups fresh or frozen blueberries

1. Preheat oven to 400°F. Grease a 12-cup muffin tin or line it with fluted-paper cups.
2. Combine flour, sugar, baking powder, and salt in a large bowl using a whisk.
3. Combine eggs, milk, butter, and vanilla in another bowl using a whisk.
4. Stir the wet ingredients into the dry ingredients; then fold in blueberries with a spatula. Fill muffin cups with the batter, distributing the batter evenly.
5. Sprinkle tops with sugar. Bake 15 minutes.

"It's not easy being a mother. If it were easy, fathers would do it."

—DOROTHY ON *THE GOLDEN GIRLS*

SAY BEDTIME PRAYERS

There's nothing sweeter than watching your children say a bedtime prayer.

Grace

BY E. RUTTER LEATHAM

Thank you for the world so sweet,
Thank you for the food we eat.
Thank you for the birds that sing,
Thank you, God, for everything.

Now I Lay Me Down

Now I lay me down to sleep,
I pray the Lord my soul to keep,
Lord, be with me through the night
And keep me 'til the morning light.

A Child's Evening Hymn

I hear no voice, I feel no touch,
I see no glory bright;
But yet I know that God is near,
In darkness as in light.
God watches ever by my side,
And hears my whispered prayer:
A God of love for a little child
Both night and day does care.

Angel Blessing at Bedtime

Angels bless and angels keep
Angels guard me while I sleep
Bless my heart and bless my home
Bless my spirit as I roam
Guide and guard me through the night
And wake me with the morning's light.
Amen.

Printed in the United States
By Bookmasters